A Distant Time and Place

Starting life as a member of a family of largely waterside workers during the depression of the1930s, Frank Vincent AO QC went on to become a judge in the Victorian Court of Appeal and University Chancellor. As a barrister, he practised principally in the criminal law in Victoria and for Aboriginal accused in the Northern Territory, representing over 200 men and women charged with murder. He later became Principal Judge in Crime in the Supreme Court and Chair of the Adult Parole Board.

For Angelique, Jack, Finn, and Tom –
offered in the hope that our story will
resonate helpfully in your own lives

A Distant Time and Place

FRANK VINCENT

Published by Hybrid Publishers

Melbourne Victoria Australia

www.hybridpublishers.com.au

First published 2020

A catalogue record for this
book is available from the
National Library of Australia

ISBN 9781925736434

Cover design: Gittus Graphics www.gggraphics.com.au

CONTENTS

INTRODUCTION

Usually, when it has been suggested that I write something of my personal history, I have responded by saying I was unsure whether I would be prepared to set out the truth even if I was confident that I could identify it.

Personal narratives almost always contain fictional elements or, at least, unfortunate self-enhancing exaggerations. Understandably, we are inclined too often to present ourselves, to ourselves, as heroes and victims, happy to claim credit for successes but less so as contributors to our own misfortunes. Nor are we disposed to emphasise the role that luck or support from others has played in our achievements. Typical experiences and common life challenges tend to be portrayed as exceptional or as incredible obstacles that have been courageously overcome, with features that might detract from the desired image likely to be omitted or downplayed. And there are always elements of our personalities, and incidents in our past about which we are not proud and that we prefer to leave there.

Given these reservations, why then did I finally decide to make this attempt? I am still not sure, but I think it lies in a wish to leave some trace of Dawn and myself as real people who struggled, lived and loved, but in a very different time and place. I offer what I see as an impressionistic tapestry of our lives with many threads lost, a few omitted, and some of the colours faded through time, but one that hopefully conveys an essentially true image.

— Frank Vincent, 2020

DAWN

I was just twenty-two when I started as a first-year solicitor at the firm of Holding, Ryan and Co. in Melbourne. Clyde Holding was an aspiring politician, yet to obtain a seat in parliament and eager for any opportunity to build his connections. He suggested I work for him, primarily, I suspect, because my father was an official of one of the maritime unions and Holding wanted to consolidate his relationship with it for political and business reasons.

The office to which I was taken was small but bright and newly furnished. A nameplate, I was told, would soon be put on the door. I was really happy as I sat behind the desk and commenced to read the case files left for my attention. Delighted by my new status, I was more than a little self-impressed.

That was certainly the view formed by my secretary when she introduced herself. Her name was Dawn. She was sixteen years of age and stunningly beautiful. At the time, there was no way of anticipating she would soon become the person around whom my life would continue to revolve. It is appropriate to start with that meeting because, although this is my story, it is also a part of hers.

MY BACKGROUND

In 1937 when I entered the world, Port Melbourne, where my parents lived, was a working-class waterfront suburb. From this distance in time and society, the difficult situation of those who lived there might not be easy to appreciate. It arose mostly from long-existing widespread poverty in the area that had been generally worsened by the Great Depression of the 1930s, but also from an industrial conflict that impacted especially heavily on the residents.

A great many of the local men, including several of my uncles and cousins, were members of a union called the Waterside Workers' Federation and depended for their livelihood on engagement as casual labourers, loading and unloading ships. The work was poorly paid, physically demanding and dangerous. Much of the cargo had to be manhandled into position in large nets and heavy bags that they were required to manually drag and push or carry on their backs.

Until the Second World War, even the process of securing this employment was demeaning. Those seeking a job would assemble each morning and afternoon in an open area exposed to the weather near the wharf entrance. They would then be selected like cattle under the appropriately named 'bull system', with the observably stronger, and those prepared to pay a bribe, chosen first. It was not a form of employment to pursue if other options were available.

Later, I developed and have maintained a deep respect for these men and their families. This has not been due to some form of romantic attachment or nostalgia about my past, or to some need to emphasise how far I have travelled. Instead, it rests upon an appreciation of the nature of their struggle and my strong commitment never to forget the values and understandings gained from this background.

Only nine years before I was born, a waterfront dispute arising from a new industrial award that reduced the working conditions further had led to a protracted strike. Although the stock market collapse that is usually regarded as marking the onset of the Depression did not occur until late in 1928, a downturn in trade had already begun. The bulk of the lessening work was being allocated to an organisation which employers had established from the increasing ranks of the unemployed in an attempt to break union resistance. Most of the men who remained loyal to the WWF had been without income for two months.

Consequently, emotions were running high on 4 November 1928 when union members assembled at the pick-up area to seek work and protest the use of the new labour force. As might be expected, a confrontation developed between them and the police who were barring their entry to the wharf where equally desperate men were loading a ship. It culminated in violence, with one protesting union member, Alan Whittaker, being fatally shot by police and two others wounded. Many years later, I reviewed the unsatisfactory inquest into Whittaker's death which, I concluded, had resulted from a loss of self-control by the officer in charge of the police detachment.

The medical evidence indicates that Whittaker was facing away from the police when he was struck in the neck by a bullet that entered from behind and exited through his cheek. He was almost certainly hit accidentally by a ricochet as he tried to move away when the firing started. On admission to hospital, he was recorded as being in generally poor physical condition, malnourished and with rotten teeth, resulting in septicaemia and his death, ironically on Australia Day, a little less than three months later.

Understandably, Whittaker's fellow unionists viewed him as just another impoverished man who was killed while walking what was later described as the 'hungry mile' in their company. That expression originated in Sydney where workers would go from wharf to wharf in search of a job, often failing to find one. The situation was worsened by the knowledge that Whittaker had been wounded on the beach at Gallipoli during the initial landing in 1915, which had left him with a pronounced limp.

The shooting of the protesting unionists became highly politicised, and there were calls for a full inquiry into the circumstances. However, this did not eventuate and the issues were never resolved. In consequence, there was both long-lasting bitterness and a powerful culture of community and union solidarity in Port Melbourne. The few residents who, for reasons of economic necessity, decided to defect to the new body were ostracised and left the suburb, while the circumstances of those who stayed loyal to the union worsened.

Even when the work situation improved substantially with the increased demand for labour after the outbreak of the Second World War, recovery from the Depression for many of the people in Port Melbourne was protracted. One of the long-lasting consequences of this period was the development of a level of militancy in the waterfront unions that has affected labour relations to the present day. It also had significant impact upon my family's situation and perspectives.

JOHN AND SUZANNAH

My father was a descendant of a Cornish man, John Vincent, and his wife, Suzannah, who arrived as free settlers with five children in Hobart Town, Van Diemen's Land, on the merchant ship *Elizabeth* in 1823. This was only twenty years after the founding of the colony as a remote penal settlement. John's family had been long-established landowners and successful farmers in the Callington area of Cornwall, and he was described as a builder.

According to family history, Suzannah was the illegitimate daughter of George Pitt, the elder brother of William Pitt, Prime Minister of England. As far as I am aware, no record of her birth has been found, but George did have at least one child by the woman believed to be Suzannah's mother; it was a male who, after achieving great success in the army, was recognised by the family. So, it is possible, as I understand from one of my relatives who conducted extensive research into the family's history and established contact with them, that our connection has been accepted by Pitt descendants in England. It seems Suzannah's mother was not regarded as a socially acceptable marriage partner for George, and it is noteworthy that neither ever married.

I have always been intrigued that a well-off man in John Vincent's position would take his wife and several children on a long and dangerous journey to a raw and recently established penal colony on the other side of the world. It is claimed within the family that he was paid to take Suzannah and the children away, which could well have been the case, as this was a known method of dealing with embarrassing situations at the time. Whether this is the explanation for their arrival in the colony or whether John saw opportunities beyond those available to him in England—which I think is more likely—is unknown. Settlement of the new lands was being actively encouraged by the United Kingdom Government with land grants and support, and, as his activities on arrival demonstrated, he was entrepreneurial and hard working.

Official records show that, however he came by them, John had the current equivalent of $700,000 when he arrived, a huge amount at that time and, with the strong support of the Governor, he was quite successful. He constructed and operated several hotels, some of which are still standing, and a mill that is now a heritage site, although not always (according to those same records) in conformity with the law. He was, more than once, charged with breaching the liquor laws and, even in that robust society, regarded as unsuitable for appointment as a Justice of the Peace. John was not, it seems, a particularly nice character. He repeatedly complained about the standard of the convict labour supplied for his various projects, and I have been told of his disgraceful treatment of the local Aboriginal people. He participated in their violent expulsion from traditional areas to accommodate the expansion of the settlements.

Even for a family as well placed as his, life in the colony must have been difficult, particularly for women. Their histories were seldom well recorded, as is the case for Suzannah. However, we do know that she was the victim of a robbery under arms by a group of escaped bushranging convicts at one of the hotels John built on the outskirts of the settlement. She was the principal witness against them at their trial, and they were hanged.

By the time my father was born in a tiny worker's cottage in the goldmining town of Beaconsfield in 1910, only the history of this affluence remained. There is a distinct possibility that one of his uncles had attempted to partially replenish the family coffers through his participation in a robbery of the town bank, although he was acquitted by a local jury on the alibi evidence of relatives. Claiming to be affronted by newspaper reports that suggested he was involved, he sued for defamation and recovered damages. Either he had been severely wronged or he had remarkable *chutzpah.* I suspect the latter as he was a reputed gambler.

My paternal grandfather, Frank Vincent, started his apprenticeship as a blacksmith at the age of nine and worked at that trade throughout his life, first in the goldfields and later in railway workshops. My legacy from him is a cargo hook he made for my father that I always proudly kept in my chambers when I was a barrister and judge.

EDMUND O'KEEFFE

My paternal grandmother was a daughter of Edmund O'Keeffe, who had been evicted with his family from their home in Ireland during land clearing in the 1840s and later settled in the Westbury district in Tasmania. Edmund's role in the escape to America of two of the Irish nationalists who had been transported for treason against the British Crown, Thomas Meagher and John Mitchel, was the subject of considerable family pride. Edmund was described by Mitchel as 'Meagher's faithful companion and guide' and as:

> a well-informed man who emigrated to Van Diemen's land after Lord Harwarden's great extermination of tenantry in Tipperary. O'Keefe was one of the tenants turned out, he saw his house pulled down, while his neighbours were warned not to shelter him or any members of his family. With the help of some good friends he found means to emigrate and now has a good farm ...

Why Edmund and his family were singled out in this way—with others being warned not to assist him—and why friends in that impoverished country rallied to the family's support and secured the necessary funds to enable them to leave—is not recorded.

He almost certainly had a connection with the Irish Republican Brotherhood, as that group organised both escapes. When helping Mitchel, Edmund, who was for some reason under suspicion at the time, had to evade police surveillance and travel overland in terrible conditions. At night in midwinter he then took Mitchel with

two companions through what Mitchel described as:

> Wild and impervious country as I have ever seen—no mountains, but countless hills, divided almost uniformly by dangerous marshes, rocks, dead trees, deep creeks with rotten banks, such, without intermission for forty miles … We came into a narrow gorge, very rocky and entangled with almost impassable scrub. Down the gorge oozed, through slimy soil and prostrate decayed trees, a kind of creek which we must cross; but never in all my bush riding had I seen so hideous and perilous-looking a task for a horseman.

They reached the comparative safety of the home of another conspirator and, soon after, Mitchel was smuggled to the United States.

MY FATHER

In addition to my father, there were four other children in his family—two boys and two girls. As far as I am aware, none of them had much education, and he himself had minimal reading and writing skills. Nevertheless, he completed an indentured hairdressing apprenticeship, and I was told he was working in a hospital in Victoria when he was attacked and slashed with his own razor by a patient. My father never returned to hairdressing but picked up short-term labouring jobs whenever he could.

Securing work of this kind became more and more difficult for him as economic conditions deteriorated during the 1930s. He told me that, during one short period, he earned money 'shoddy dropping'—a term given to the selling of small household items door-to-door. At another time when his situation was particularly difficult, he tried his hand as a pool-hall hustler, betting on the outcome of games. This was an unreliable and sometimes dangerous way to make a living, because he seldom would have been able to cover his bet if he had lost. He was amused by an occasion when he discovered the person he was playing was also a hustler with no money.

My father developed techniques to conceal his low level of literacy, and for many years engaged in trade union politics and the Australian Labor Party. His success in these areas was almost certainly due to his remarkable ability as a public speaker and as a shrewd and capable advocate for his members. He also had considerable personal presentational skills. He said it is important to appear comfortable and quietly strong rather than arrogant or aggressive if you wish to be taken seriously by the organisations and individuals you have to deal with. You should have at least one good suit and a pair of highly polished shoes so you would 'look the part'. It was an approach he certainly adopted himself. The only advice he gave to Dawn when we were married was to remind me to keep my shoes in good order.

Although my father held various positions with the Waterside Workers' Federation over the years, he was seldom paid for any of them and worked 'under the hook' throughout—that is, as a waterfront labourer.

To compensate for his limited literacy skills, I was introduced to political and industrial issues from a very early age and required to read, and even compose, political material for him, including pamphlets for union elections. He would explain what was involved and what he wanted to say, and I would set it out for him. I particularly liked working on pamphlets which were directed to convey resonating messages as economically as possible.

I was thirteen when I first became involved in this way in a major political campaign: the referendum that followed the declaration by the High Court of Australia in March 1951 that legislation passed by the Commonwealth Parliament to ban the Communist Party of Australia was unconstitutional. The prospect that, under the new powers being sought, my father could be required to denounce some of his workmates was of grave concern. Through his role as Vice President of the Trades Hall Council in northern Tasmania and as an active trade unionist, he knew and worked with many communists at both the state and national level. He was a typical left-wing working-class Catholic of the period and rejected their doctrines, but did not doubt they were motivated by a genuine desire to improve the living standards and opportunities for the poor in our society.

My parents and I discussed his situation and accepted that he would refuse to comply with requests for information about his various associations. We understood this could well have serious consequences for us. Wanting to do what I could, I attended meetings, read extensively on the issues, delivered pamphlets door-to-door after school on my bike, and handed out how-to-vote cards on polling day at the local high school. That night we listened anxiously to the tally on the radio. Fortunately for Australian democracy, the proposal was rejected.

From his early fifties, my father's health began to deteriorate. He handled this with remarkable stoicism until his death at the age of sixty-one. At one point, when discussing the prospects of a heart operation he was to undergo, he said in his laconic manner, 'The quack said that its fours on, but there's no second dividend [The doctor said there is an eighty per cent chance of success but a twenty per cent risk of death].' He survived the operation but soon afterwards lost the bet.

Towards the end of his life, he secured light duties at a ferry terminal servicing King Island in Bass Strait where, in typical waterfront style, he was known as 'the Judge', his workmates affectionately claiming he could usually be found 'sitting on a case' directing operations and giving advice rather than helping to move them. Nicknames of that kind were common. One was called 'Glass-Arm Harry' and another, 'the London Fog'. Both, it seemed, had difficulty with lifting. They were a roughly spoken, decent bunch, and, as a young lawyer, I would sometimes call in at the terminal or meet them in one of the local pubs if I had been working in a nearby court. The son of one them later became a County Court judge.

MY MOTHER

My mother was born Una Yendall in Port Melbourne, also in 1910. Her father was an Anglican of Cornish origin and a descendant of William George Yendall, who initially came to Australia as a twenty-year-old soldier, guarding convicts held at the Port Arthur Penitentiary or as workers provided for the free settlers, and then as a Governor's aide. There is, I think, a high probability that he would have encountered, or at least known of, John Vincent.

George had joined the army as a young man to avoid personal difficulties in which he found himself. The circumstances can only be speculated about from the description he provided in a memoir for his family:

> I began to think myself something amongst the females and they themselves thought I was one to be admired but betwixt myself and them I got entangled in so much that I was in a fix. What to do to clear myself I scarcely knew. I came to the conclusion that I would leave home and I was not certain whether I should be traced or not.

His solution was to seek refuge in an organisation that took him far away. He remained in the army for over twenty-one years, and during his service fought in many battles in India and Burma where:

> [t]here were more British soldiers lost by hard marching and privations, hunger and thirst than fell by the enemy … we would be marching in the burning heat and when

> we had done our day's march perhaps there would be a bit of salt pork—cook it the best way we could, and nothing but the canopy of heaven to cover you. We had to drink the water from the river in which the dead were thrown and also dead cattle … Our greatest enemy was starvation.

Later, he returned to Australia where he finally settled. My grandfather, also called William George, was a plumber by trade and worked in a sugar refinery throughout my mother's childhood.

Her mother, an observant Catholic, was proud of her Irish descent, but I know almost nothing about her. Regrettably, as I have already mentioned, women's histories were seldom recorded in any detail and I have only an image of a woman who was proud of her Irish background and loved music and dancing. It is doubtful that she had a continuing association with her own family, as my mother never mentioned having met any. She told me that some of my grandmother's relatives were members of the Catholic clergy, while my grandfather's family were staunchly Anglican. In those days, for my grandparents to have married outside their respective church affiliations would have been viewed with extreme disapproval on both sides and such severance could be expected.

There were six children in my mother's family, with the four eldest raised as Anglicans. My mother and her sister Iris were baptised as Catholics, and this led to some tension and dispute over her education. More than once, she was enrolled in the same local parish school I would later attend, and then removed by her father. At my grandmother's initiative, Iris and my mother learned tap dancing, and they regularly appeared together in variety shows that played around the suburbs and provided a major source of entertainment for people in the early 1920s.

My mother always claimed her early life was happy despite the issues with her education. But I wonder if that was the case or whether it just appeared so in comparison with the difficult period that followed. She was only fifteen when Iris and she left home to tour as the Nuttall sisters, singing and dancing in a travelling magic show in country towns across Victoria and southern New South Wales. Nothing was ever said as to how that came about, and it is surprising that two teenage girls, particularly one as young as my mother, were engaged in this type of activity and an almost certainly dangerous life in 1925.

My mother's parents died within three months of each other only a short time later when she was sixteen. She stayed with one of her older brothers for some months, but it seems her sister-in-law resented her presence and my mother soon had to fend for herself. She said little about her late teenage and early adult years during the Depression, and I formed the impression that times were very hard for her. She did tell me that she worked in different jobs, including factory hand, live-in maid and, later, as a florist. She was artistic, and in that last job, she learned how to make almost every imaginable flower or leaf from coloured crepe paper that she would then wax and arrange in beautiful displays for our home.

One of my mother's defining characteristics was an intense fear of poverty. As a teenager and a single young woman, she had survived mostly on her own during the depths of the Depression and had seen people forcibly evicted from their homes, their few belongings thrown onto the street. She was one of a group of 'bailiff runners': young people organised by Jenny Baines, a former suffragette from England, to go from house to house calling out residents to act as human barricades to prevent such evictions. My mother also assisted Jenny in anti-poverty campaigns and told me of one occasion when she was dressed in waif-like rags and taken as part of a deputation to the State Premier's office.

Jenny was one of my mother's real heroes. Her history was extraordinary and involved many periods of imprisonment over her life as she fought against the injustice and inequality that surrounded her, particularly in relation to women. My mother introduced me to her when I was quite young, and I would regularly call in at her house on my way home from school. Jenny always made me feel welcome and encouraged me in my schoolwork. I feel privileged to have known her.

These experiences had a powerful impact upon my mother. Throughout my childhood, payment of the rent was treated as a first priority, as shelter was seen as the most basic need. She reasoned that, provided that was secured, it would always be possible to secure sufficient of the other necessities for the family to survive. Furniture and other large or expensive items were purchased one at a time on lay-by or hire-purchase arrangements so that, if she was unable to keep up payments, only one item would be lost.

In consequence of my mother's underlying fear, the kitchen cupboards in our home were always filled with canned food. This was just one of a range of strategies she employed to ensure we would be well fed and properly clothed. She would purchase whatever was on sale and store it against the future. Industrial disputes created particular difficulties for my parents. They were of the view that there were others worse off than ourselves and that my father should not accept the small amounts of money distributed to union members as 'strike pay', or receive any of the food collected to assist families if we could manage without it, and we always did.

One of my strongest images of my mother relates to an event on my seventh birthday. It was wartime, and she had saved enough ration coupons for ice creams and lemonade for everyone at my party. One boy had no present for me, so he gave me his own rusty toy gun. She took me to one side and carefully explained that, because he had given what he had, it was the most important gift I had received and should be valued. I kept that gun for a long time.

Another concerns a story she impressed upon me and has resonated throughout my life. She claimed she knew of a young boy in England who had secured a scholarship to attend a prestigious school. When he arrived on the first morning and heard, from across the street, the upper-class accents of his fellow students, and observed their comfortable familiarity with both the environment and each other, he felt so out of place that he went home and never returned. Her message was clear: it must never happen to me. I must never back away for any reason related to societal position or status or defer to privilege.

My mother was a strong-minded woman and a proud survivor who, like my father, was deeply committed to her family. He would laughingly say that, if necessary, he would walk through hell with his boots off for us, and I never doubted him. Nor did I ever doubt that she would have walked with him, if not in front.

She was always interested in the theatre and was in her seventies when, although not in good health, she secured an agent and started working as an extra in television and movie productions, often as a derelict old lady in an alley or dark street. One role that really delighted her was in a comedy film where she was dressed in a nineteenth-century crinoline and chased up a hill by a camel. When I pointed out that this was madness for a woman who was almost ninety, she said 'there are worse ways to go.'

PORT MELBOURNE

My parents met in 1936 and married in December of that year at St Joseph's Church in Port Melbourne. Their wedding reception was held at a local hall and catered for in the fashion of the suburb by gifts from friends. She would often relate with great delight that they had so much food that, at the end, local unemployed people were invited in to share it.

Not long after I was born, they decided to move to Burnie, Tasmania, where one of my father's brothers operated a funeral director's business, as they thought he had a better chance of securing regular work there. This proved to be the case; after several months, he joined the Waterside Workers' Federation, working on the small coastal vessels that carried much of the cargo around northern Tasmania and the Bass Strait islands. There was still not a great deal of work available and, with the help of crew members, he would stow away in ships' chain lockers and load or unload as needed at each port. We stayed in Burnie for two years before he was able to transfer back to Victoria under the union rules.

Shortly after our return, we moved into a single-fronted terrace house in Graham Street, Port Melbourne, where we lived for the remainder of our time in the suburb. Our home, which was typical of the area and identical to the others in the row, had four small rooms, a laundry with a wood-burning copper for clothes washing and hot water for the tin bath, and an outside toilet in the backyard. Three nearby houses in the street were occupied by members of my mother's family, and all the men worked on the wharves. Almost all my early childhood memories are of the time we lived there.

Port Melbourne during the Second World War and early postwar period was a busy place with cargo, troop and hospital ships, and factories. There were soldiers and sailors everywhere. Some were connected with a naval base, HMAS *Lonsdale*, about a hundred metres from our home. A large coal-operated gasworks was located a little further on and, two blocks in the opposite direction, a church was used as a refugee centre for people from Java in what were then the Dutch East Indies. Open-top slit trenches with wooden side supports had been dug on several nearby vacant blocks, and we would often play in them.

For me, war and the bravery of our soldiers were epitomised by a friend of my father who I remember as a tall, powerfully built man, but of course, may simply have appeared so to a young boy. He was a romantic figure with a long shrapnel scar on his face from his service as one of the legendary Rats of Tobruk who had fought valiantly against the German Afrika Korps in North Africa. However, the price many had to pay did not entirely escape me. Glimpses could be seen in the lines of ambulances that I watched travelling from the hospital ships berthed at Station Pier as I walked to school.

I began to follow the progress of the allied forces in Europe, particularly the massive movements on the Eastern Front, and kept a scrapbook of maps that I cut out from the newspapers. I thought the dropping of a 'super bomb' on a Japanese city was wonderful, but at seven years of age, I had no understanding of the horror of the event. When the bells, car horns and sirens announced the Japanese surrender on VJ Day, another boy and I hoisted an Australian flag on his woodshed roof, and my mother took me to the city to join in the celebrations.

*

In retrospect, Port Melbourne was probably a quite unsafe area to wander around as freely as I did, but I am sure my mother, who had lived there most of her life, never saw it as such. She claimed that, with so many relatives and friends nearby, I was never at risk. Perhaps she was right—and there were certainly plenty of people about who knew our family. At my insistence, I was allowed to walk to school on my own from the age of five, although I later learned she used to follow me from a distance for some time.

I was about nine when I started going to the Saturday afternoon movies in South Melbourne with other Port Melbourne kids. We sometimes found ourselves involved in running fist fights and stone throwing with groups we encountered on the way to the theatre which was regarded as neutral territory where fights were not allowed. These battles were seen as part of the adventure and I enjoyed them, but they could be dangerous. During one of them, I felled a member of the opposing group with a large piece of house brick. He received a cut on his head, but got up and ran off with his friends. I thought nothing of it.

During the warmer months, I could usually be found at the beach, swimming or diving for mussels around the piers. I would take a hessian sugar bag and dive down, pulling them from the pylons or cutting them free with a knife that I had tied to a waist strap.

After receiving a bike for Christmas when I was ten, my horizons expanded, and I often rode with other boys to St Kilda where we would sneak onto the foreshore carnival rides until we were chased off. It was a great game but also probably risky for more than one reason. There is a good chance that we were observed by any potential predators and I have no doubt that there were some about, as we were a group of tough, scruffy kids left to our own devices. In any event, we moved freely and without trouble.

Saturday afternoons provided lots of entertainment. There

were frequent brawls in and around the Graham Family Hotel, a few doors from our home, and one of my adult cousins who had a substantial reputation in the area as a street fighter was involved in many of them. The local kids would sit on the footpath on the opposite side of the road and watch what were sometimes brutal confrontations. Losers were often thrown into a horse-watering trough outside the hotel, but I have seen my cousin use it to wash blood from his face before returning to the fight.

Domestic violence was commonplace. One afternoon when some boys and I were playing on a nearby football oval, a man who lived in the adjoining street and who I had seen many times, arrived home carrying several bottles of beer in his arms. Unusually, he was sober and deeply affronted when his wife, as customary, appeared a short time later, very drunk. After a noisy argument in which he expressed outrage at her state, she ran down the street as he hurled bottles after her. It probably says something about the general social environment that the terrible character of what was happening didn't occur to us, and we enjoyed watching the bottles explode as they struck the ground. The man then sat on the gutter edge and commenced to drink the remainder. His wife joined him, and peace was restored.

There were two illegal bookmakers operating close to our home. One had set up in a lane across the road, and I was sometimes sent there to place small bets for my father. The betting sheets were fixed to a fence and could be pivoted out of sight in the event of a police raid. There always seemed to be plenty of time to do this before they appeared. The other one also operated openly behind a small transmission station in the next street.

An illegal 'two-up school', a traditional gambling game played with two pennies, was held in the dressing shed at the local football oval each weekend. We liked seeing the players scatter just before the police arrived. Obviously, they were tipped off. One morning before the game started, I hid a jar in the shed containing a small amount of iron sulphide and hydrochloric acid. The rotten egg smell of the hydrogen sulphide was dreadful, and the men searched for the cause. They never found the jar and almost certainly gave no thought to the possibility that the kids playing nearby had anything to do with ruining their afternoon.

I was interested in science and built on the chemistry set my parents had given me as a present on my eighth birthday. A paint factory I passed on my way to school was a primary source of materials, including test tubes and other glassware. I would call in to watch the testing of the various products, and the men would give me small amounts for my experiments. By the time I was in what I thought would be my final school year in Tasmania, I had accumulated an impressive range of laboratory equipment and materials. Fortunately, I didn't poison or injure myself or anyone else, although I did make an effective rat poison at one stage.

It was while we were living in Port Melbourne that my father made the first of two attempts at establishing a business, manufacturing and selling hair oil and perfume. He bought a large quantity of bottles from a man who claimed that, as an employee of the bottle manufacturer, he could secure them at a substantial discount. When my father learned they had been stolen, he was horrified. Not only were they unusable but he was worried that his explanation of innocent purchase would not be accepted if they were found in his possession. So, the pair of us set about smashing them with hammers. We placed the fragments in sacks and threw them off the end of a pier. He didn't have the money to buy replacements. He tried again later when we were living in Tasmania, but having little capital, was unable to make a success of it.

This venture also led to my first solo trip to the city. My father was at work, and I was sent to buy a gallon of pure alcohol for perfume. He had the necessary licence, which I produced at the wholesalers, but it is surprising that, even then, a boy of my age would be entrusted with such a task and even more extraordinary that the alcohol would be given to him. I carried it home on the bus.

The wartime rationing of some food items, such as meat, butter and tea, as well as new clothing, presented a significant challenge for my mother. She would walk three kilometres from our home to the South Melbourne Market, where she would buy second-hand books and clothing as well as most of our vegetables. Shirts would be cut down and sewn to fit us. Jumpers and cardigans would be unravelled and the wool reused. Once, she acquired some parachute silk that she used for making shirts. My mother also bought leather and a bootmaker's last that my father and she used to repair our shoes. Her purchases would be transported in a pram, usually with my little brother, Brian, who was born in 1944, perched on top.

Horse-drawn carts were still commonly used by sellers of household items. Our bread, milk and ice were delivered in this way and the 'rabbit-oh' appeared in the street every couple of days. This had started during the Depression years when groups of union members were organised to go shooting for rabbits (locally called 'underground mutton') to be distributed among the unemployed. My mother regularly bought two that she would choose carefully, and he would skin them for her.

Heating their homes was never an issue for the people of Graham Street as there was a plentiful supply of coal spilled onto the road from trucks as they turned into our street on their way to the gas works. Wood for kindling could be secured from a local box factory and a billy cart of coke could also be purchased for sixpence or a shilling, according to size, at the gasworks.

PERSPECTIVE

Viewed at this range, it may appear that life during my early years in such an environment was relatively hard. By many standards, I suppose it was, but this is not how it seemed to me at the time, or now. I lived in a family that was, in many respects, indistinguishable from those around it. Although I was aware that outside the community of Port Melbourne there were well-off people who owned the houses we lived in and the companies that employed the men, I had only vague images of their lifestyles and knew nothing of what that meant in terms of the choices available to them or their day-to-day experiences. It wasn't until my teenage years that I began to gain a sense of the significance of these differences and the injustice of entrenched inequality.

My reservations about setting down something of my history have been due in part to a concern that my background will be misinterpreted as one of disadvantage. In most important senses, that was not the case. We had little money and our living conditions were poor, but I was barely aware of that and lived in a stable, loving family. My parents equipped me, not only to survive in what was for them a hostile world, but to succeed in it, and with a social understanding that many others I encountered in my professional activities were never required to possess. This proved to be a considerable advantage in my later work in the law and in life generally.

However, mine was also a real working-class family, and conditions were often difficult for my parents, particularly my mother.

They were not made any easier for her when my father, like many of the other men in the area, from time to time, would arrive home extremely drunk. He could become nasty, and I would let her know we were in for trouble as soon as I saw him walking unevenly from the bus. He was never physically abusive, but he would rant and smash things in frustration. Occasionally, when he was particularly bad, my mother would send me to the local presbytery to bring the parish priest.

My father did not behave in this way often, but he seemed to have an uncanny ability to pick the worst times to do so. On the night before my first university exam, he put on a dreadful performance that went on for hours. I was already feeling nervous and had developed painful boils on the back of my neck that had been treated at the Royal Melbourne Hospital on my way home earlier that day. As a result, I was unable to sleep and went to the exam physically and emotionally exhausted. I passed but did not do as well as I had hoped.

Given their circumstances, my parents regarded education as the only practical avenue available for advancement for their children. They wanted to ensure that we would never be restricted to the kind of work available to them. My father used to say that the dignity of labour existed only in the minds of those who never engaged in it. He certainly found none. He achieved his satisfaction in what he described as 'closing the door': the pride in being able to return home at the end of a workday and close it with his family safe and warm inside. A great deal could be tolerated to accomplish that. How small it makes the grandiose ambitions and successes of much lesser men and women.

I came to appreciate that the respect due to people like my parents doesn't arise from the nature of the work in which they engage, nor is it diminished by their low social status or income level. It is based upon the perseverance and sometimes great personal courage required as they struggle to survive and support and provide for those who depend on them.

I saw many examples of that kind of courage displayed later in workers compensation cases. For some, merely trying to work so they could support their families involved incredible self-denial and the acceptance of a serious risk of death or injury, personal hardship and humiliation, or years of tedious, stressful employment.

By contrast, I used to find myself intensely irritated when prisoners I was interviewing for parole tried to rely upon their expressed concern about the situations in which their families were placed while they were in gaol. They had failed them miserably, often for years, and I could see no indication they would not do so again. Sometimes prisoners would become angry when I challenged their claimed concern by asking confronting questions about how they had manifested their commitment to that time and why I should accept that anything had changed.

SCHOOL

Due to my father's inability to assist and his personal embarrassment, responsibility for our formal education was left to our mother. She was proud of the fact that she had secured her Merit Certificate—this was obtained at eighth grade—and encouraged me to learn from a very early age. She taught me to read, write and do some simple maths well before I started first grade at St Joseph's in Bay Street, Port Melbourne, at five years of age. An earlier attempt to start me at school was abandoned as I found the sight of nuns dressed in their habits scary and hid under a desk.

The school was operated by the Brigidine Sisters, and the elderly nun in charge had taught my mother as a child. Fees were set on a sliding scale—threepence per week for very poor or large families and sixpence for the others. We paid sixpence. My mother was delighted when, at the end of my first year, I progressed directly to third grade.

Not long before I commenced fifth grade, my parents went to a trotting race meeting, and my mother, who rarely placed a bet, won the equivalent of almost two weeks of my father's income. In typical fashion, she decided to use the money for my education and took it to the Christian Brothers College in Middle Park. I enjoyed the two and a half years I spent there before we moved to Launceston in Tasmania in 1949. My brother Brian, who was then only seven years old, joined me in my last year. I would take him to and from school, sitting precariously on the crossbar of my bike.

LAUNCESTON

The move to Launceston was made because my grandfather was unwell and my father wanted to be near him. Unfortunately, he passed away not long after we arrived, but I remember him as a thin man with a leathery face and the hardened hands of a blacksmith. He lived in a lovely old house on a steep hillside overlooking the city, with fruit trees, berry bushes and a huge walnut tree in the garden. Brian and I had great fun there.

We lived in one of the main streets behind a small watchmaker's shop conducted by an uncle by marriage. He taught me how to replace broken springs, adjust and clean watches and clocks; abilities I have long since lost. Entry to our part of the building was effected from the rear through an unlit lane behind a hotel that I found rather frightening, as I would sometimes have to pass by the shapes of people in the dark. There was a small metal fabrication business on the other side of the lane where they made spouting and pipes from galvanised iron. This was delivered in bundles of sheets surrounded by a wooden framework which it was one of my household duties to collect and cut up for firewood.

Our living area was quite decrepit: bitterly cold in winter and the roof in the bedroom I shared with Brian always leaked, despite several attempts to fix it. We used to huddle together in my single bed to keep warm and often waited for our father to put his overcoat over us after he arrived home from an evening shift. I was delighted when, years later, Dawn and I had central heating installed. From my perspective, this was a powerful symbol of success because it meant our girls need never be cold at night.

The rooms were dark and furnished with what would now be regarded as some remarkable and probably valuable nineteenth century antiques, including a vast ornate cabinet. Its possible value was lost on me and I found the whole atmosphere creepy, especially when the furniture created shadows or the many old clocks stored under our staircase began to chime when disturbed by rats.

We had no hot-water service, so my mother heated water in the kitchen on a large cast-iron stove, on which she also did most of the cooking. Because the floor had partially collapsed on one side, the table was perched on wooden blocks to keep it level. Our clothes were washed in a wood-burning copper, in an old laundry room with a concrete trough and crumbling brick walls located outside at the back. It was also used to heat water for a rusty tin bath in the same room.

My parents' financial position remained difficult during our time in Tasmania. Launceston was a small river port, servicing the northern part of the State and the Bass Strait islands. Waterside workers were engaged on a casual basis when required, and there were frequent periods when little employment was available. At those times, we resorted to my mother's hoard of tinned food or to meals prepared from sheep or pigs' heads and lamb shanks, which were very cheap. Much later, when lamb shanks appeared on the lunch menu in Barristers' Chambers, I couldn't imagine choosing them.

ST PATRICK'S COLLEGE

St Patrick's College, when I started part way through year seven, was a small school in Launceston and not, I suspect, regarded as a desirable posting for the Christian Brothers who were sent there. Being eager and encouraged by my parents, I began to spend a lot of time immersed in books from the public library only a block from my home, reading indiscriminately, but with an emphasis on history and politics. During holiday periods, as we did not go away, I would often read two or three books a day. The Second World War had only recently concluded, and I was seeking explanations of its origins that would make sense to me. This, I suppose, would be regarded as an unusual interest for a boy of my age, but I was always exposed to political and social issues, and it seemed normal.

However, my teachers were not always happy with the results of my independent studies and sometimes took exception to the 'heretical' views I expressed. They objected vehemently when I said that, given the Church's hypocrisy and abuse of power, it was hardly surprising there was such broad acceptance of Martin Luther's criticisms. They also disliked my approach in a classroom debate when I argued in favour of the retention of a then publicly owned shipping line. I thought that it was absurd for our island continent to divest itself of a guaranteed shipping connection and depend on foreign suppliers.

My external activities included regular theatre roles in local productions, often with Brian. Our mother had taught us tap dancing from an early age, and soon after we arrived in Launceston, we began to participate in children's radio programs and variety shows conducted by one of the local radio stations in halls across northern Tasmania. I cannot recall how it came about other than that it was at Brian's initiative—he would have been about nine at the time—but we started going to the station at least weekly for programs or rehearsals. We sang and danced together and participated separately in other acts.

I also appeared in some child roles in theatre productions in Hobart and Launceston. This resulted in conflict at school when, instead of participating in a religious retreat, I went to Hobart to perform in a play at the Theatre Royal. These activities were terrific fun and, as it transpired, excellent preparation for the public presentations in my later life. I lost any fear of speaking in public and learned how to 'work' an audience, remember lines and avoid the use of prompts or notes.

School holidays were mainly spent swimming and climbing around Cataract Gorge with Brian and a friend who lived nearby, or riding our bikes along the Tamar. In the summer months, we would collect wild blackberries or sit by the river eating apples from orchards we raided.

Brian and I joined the St John Ambulance Brigade together as cadets, and when I was fifteen, I became a full member. In that role, I attended road and track cycle races. On one occasion, I was on duty on my own at a country carnival when I had to treat a rider who, on falling, had driven a wooden boundary peg through his shoulder. I held him as he was transported, with the peg in place, on the tray of a truck to a hospital some kilometres away. My mother was horrified when I arrived home with my uniform covered in blood.

I also had some holiday and after-school work for which I received small amounts of money. These included washing and filling milk bottles in a dairy, sorting and loading clothes in a dry cleaner's shop and helping to fill orders in a wholesale business that supplied shops in the surrounding townships.

It was in Launceston that I first met Aboriginal people. They were either workmates of my father or crew members on the small vessels that serviced the Bass Strait islands.

My contact with them commenced when I was about twelve years old. They were among a number of men with little education that my father would bring home so I could help them prepare their income tax returns. The process was more complex than it is now, and they had difficulty completing the lengthy forms. They would bring whatever scraps of paper they had, and I would try to make sense of them as we sat in our kitchen, with my father urging me in the background to build up their deductions as much as possible. My knowledge of income tax law was not much greater than theirs, but I could at least read and complete the forms for them.

We were told at school that the last member of Tasmania's Indigenous population had died many years previously. This assertion not only failed to protect them from the racial prejudice and overt discrimination to which they were constantly subjected, but because they were denied any cultural identity or respect whatever, it aggravated their situation. Although I was vaguely aware of some of the men's Aboriginal background, I do not claim to have had any deep insight into their situation. I saw them essentially as other poor men and friends of my father.

Under the Tasmanian education system, there were five years of secondary schooling. Having already skipped second grade, this meant I was only a few months past my fifteenth birthday when I commenced my final, or matriculation, year. It also meant that I was two years younger than my class mates, a substantial difference at that age.

My ambition was to work in the rapidly developing field of

bacterial and viral disease research, but I was the only one studying science and maths at that level, and my teachers and I were clearly struggling. So, part way through the year, much to the school principal's annoyance, I enrolled in night classes at the local technical college. But I was too far behind and did poorly in the end-of-year examinations.

I became dispirited and, abandoning the idea of pursuing a career in science, I returned to school to study subjects in the humanities. I was still receiving Tasmanian Government scholarship payments, and so my fees were covered. The Principal recognised something had to be done to improve the standard, so additional after-hours classes were organised with some specialist teachers from the local high school. He also arranged employment for me with a local business to help reduce the financial pressure on my family and to encourage me to continue. That year was more successful for me, and I was granted a Commonwealth scholarship under the then recently introduced scheme that enabled me to undertake the law course at the University of Melbourne.

The decision to pursue a career in the law was to a large extent based on an image I had been developing through my early involvement in politics and industrial issues and, at that stage, I began to imagine myself grandly involved in the advancement of workers' rights. I certainly never contemplated that I would work in criminal law.

CAMP PELL

I was a few months past my seventeenth birthday when I arrived in Melbourne to commence my studies. It was an exciting time that began with my first aeroplane journey. My parents decided to move back to Victoria to support me, and also because they considered the family's prospects would be better there. This was a major decision and a gamble, particularly as Brian was only thirteen and my sister, Judith, was less than a year old. Our financial position while in Tasmania had always been difficult so they were hopeful that the increased availability of work on the Melbourne waterfront would result in improvement. While this proved to be the case, as it transpired they badly underestimated the difficulty of securing accommodation.

They arranged for me to stay with my aunt Iris and her family in their rented house in North Carlton, and soon afterwards, joined me there. It was understood that this could only be temporary as my aunt and uncle would soon be moving. In the meantime, there would be nine of us living in their tiny single-fronted terrace home.

We had hopes of staying on after they left or securing other accommodation but, within a couple of months, we were in real danger of being homeless. The owners had decided to sell—a process that was much easier with the end of the existing tenancy— and we had no right to remain. This presented the family with a serious problem. Not only were we unable to secure somewhere to live at a rental we could afford due to a continuing post-war shortage of housing generally, but most landlords wanted a security deposit we could not provide.

Almost at the last moment, my father secured a unit for us at Camp Pell. This was the name given to a Second World War American army base located in a large park just north of the city and within a short walking distance of the university, where some of the old galvanised iron huts had been converted for use as emergency accommodation. Although Camp Pell was a disgrace and had been so for a long time, it had provided essential housing for many families. After years of controversy, the camp was being closed and few new families were accepted. We were lucky in this regard as it meant that our stay was likely to be relatively short, with Housing Commission homes being provided for the remaining residents.

Camp Pell had a reputation as a dangerous place; there was great stigma attached to living there. In the newspapers, it was referred to as 'Camp Hell', 'a breeding ground of physical and spiritual disease' and a 'squalid sink-hole'. There had been repeated demands for its closure for several years as a 'government-sponsored slum'. It is indicative of the residents' public image that the parliamentary opposition leader at the time, Henry Bolte, called for a compulsory rehabilitation program to be established for the residents before they could be provided with public housing, so they would not 'turn it into a slum'. Of course, more than a few of those who lived there manifested the consequences of poverty, and some terrible things did happen, including murders and outbreaks of disease, but many were just struggling working-class people with nowhere else to live.

Coincidentally, Dawn's family had also faced housing difficulties and had lived at Camp Pell for about twelve months a couple of years earlier. For most of her first eight years, they had lived in a damp one-room bungalow at the rear of a house in Footscray. Dawn had contracted poliomyelitis when she was five, and their situation had been extremely difficult. Unable to secure other housing, they moved to Camp Pell because of a concern about her condition, in particular, the risk of pneumonia. She told me that as bad as conditions were there, they were a lot better than in the bungalow. From my perspective, although the physical conditions in the camp were bad, they did not seem significantly worse than those in which I had previously lived.

In many respects, Dawn's circumstances as a child were much more difficult than my own. Her family did not have the same economic pressures to contend with because her father was in regular employment. However, he was an alcoholic who drank every day after work and terrorised Dawn and her mother.

She attributed his behaviour to his war service and there was certainly a basis for this view. From my later observation, there would seem to be little doubt that his war service impacted heavily upon him and, of course, their lives. He had survived many battles as a machine gunner in 'island hopping' campaigns in the Pacific region as our troops forced the Japanese to retreat from the conquered areas. This was regarded as particularly hazardous duty, with life expectancy in combat assessed in minutes. In common with many returned servicemen and women, he would never talk about that period or associate with veterans' groups or any activity connected to it.

As a consequence of her polio, Dawn was also required to sleep with casts on her legs for over five years and was never allowed to engage in sport or ride a bike because of her vulnerability to injury. Her schooling was delayed; when she started at the age of seven, she was only able to attend part-time for several months.

The Camp Pell huts were divided into five small units separated by thin plaster wall partitions through which sound travelled easily.

We occupied Unit E in Hut 8, Area 5, an address I entered with a strong sense of defiance on various university forms and library cards. Our unit was partitioned into two tiny rooms that were just large enough for our beds, and a small living space with a kitchen bench and stove at one end. There was no hot water, and because of the difficulties in using the wood-fired copper located outside in an unlined galvanised iron annex that also contained our bath and toilet, my mother washed some of our clothes, particularly Judith's, in a cut-down kerosene tin on the kitchen stove. Sadly, she was used to this this from our time in Launceston. There was a communal laundry hut some distance away, but it was a nasty, dangerous place and my mother hated going there.

As might be expected in a metal army hut with no effective insulation, our unit was often stifling in summer and freezing in winter. There was an extraordinary contraption in the living area that, once filled with sawdust, would burn for hours. It produced tremendous heat but had to be carefully guarded, could not be adjusted and, for practical purposes, could not be extinguished once lit. Most of the pathways in the area were unsealed and, although boards had been laid down in some sections, dust and mud made daily life more difficult.

Not having anywhere to study at home, I would spend most nights at the law school library and walk back to the camp at about ten o'clock. After we moved to our Housing Commission home, I continued this practice, travelling on the train with the waterside workers who had just finished their evening or 'twilight' shift.

Contrary to the reputation of Camp Pell, the only violence I experienced during our time there came from the police. They would drive around the area harassing young men of my general age. On several nights, when returning to our unit after study, I was stopped and forced against a fence as they went through my bag and contemptuously tipped its contents on the ground before they left. Later, at home, I would wipe the mud or dirt from them. It never occurred to me to lodge a complaint about what I considered normal police behaviour in working-class areas. As a child, I had seen several examples of this type of conduct in Port Melbourne, including raids on homes in our street.

My last such encounter occurred a few years later. It took place shortly after I had started at the bar. One night, after leaving Dawn's home, I was walking through the Housing Commission area in which she lived towards a bus stop when I was suddenly thrown and held against a factory fence by some plain-clothes police. When, after some verbal abuse and manhandling, they discovered I was a barrister, and therefore possibly a problem, they became extremely apologetic and offered to drive me home. I let them.

Most of the camp residents moved to homes in newly constructed public housing estates in the outer suburbs. Dawn's family went to an area in the west, and we were allocated a house in Glenroy, a suburb to the north of the city, after we had been in the camp for a little under a year. These moves resulted in a considerable improvement in the living circumstances of both families. Our house was located on a large block at the edge of the estate and I established a substantial vegetable garden with fruit trees on which I worked for some time most weekends.

LAW SCHOOL

In 1955, the Melbourne University Law School had only a couple of hundred students. They generally came from well-off families and a few private schools and appeared, at least, to be very comfortable in this setting. The few who didn't fall into this group had attended a small number of high schools and knew each other, or were generally much older; a couple were members of the police force, and there were a couple of ex-servicemen who had returned to study.

Although I developed some lasting friendships at the university, particularly with another law student, Barney Cooney, who later had a distinguished career in the Australian Senate, I felt isolated there. Not only was I a socially clumsy young person with a waterfront background, living during my first year in Camp Pell and then in a Housing Commission home, but I was also from a small town in Tasmania and had no school connections or social links with any of my fellow students. There were few female law students, and I knew none in any of the other faculties. Even if there had been enough money to invite one of them to go out with me, I would not have done so, anticipating—quite reasonably I think—that they would almost certainly have viewed me as seriously 'down-market' and refused.

The Commonwealth scholarship carried a living allowance which was means-tested and sufficient to satisfy basic daily needs while living at home. Although I earned some money from odd jobs and during my obligatory periods of national service in the army, it wasn't a great deal, and almost all went on travel expenses, clothing and additional books.

My parents were doing their best for me and were very proud that I was studying to become a lawyer, so I concealed my feelings. Some Saturday nights I would tell them I was going out with friends but then take the train to the city to see a movie. There would undoubtedly have been others who had a similar experience, but issues of this kind were neither acknowledged nor discussed in that environment of intense competition and apparent self-confidence.

For equally powerful reasons, I had developed no significant friendships with any of the other young people I encountered in Camp Pell or the Glenroy area into which many had moved. This was not because I felt in some way superior to them. In many respects, I had much more in common with them than I did with the students: our paths, aspirations and interests were just too different. This never resulted in any attempt at physical intimidation by any of the local young men who, if they noticed me at all, almost certainly would simply have regarded me as an oddity. And I was never apprehensive as I moved about in an environment in which I was confident and comfortable.

I liked studying in the Supreme Court library as it was quiet and held the promise of a career to come, so I went there frequently. Although it was available only for practitioners, I was never asked to leave. During breaks, I would visit various courtrooms and sit in the public gallery watching civil and criminal hearings. I learned much about advocacy from these observations and the different approaches adopted during this period. It became obvious that there was no point in trying to emulate others—I would need to develop my own approach—drawing upon my individual abilities, understandings and personality.

A criminal trial has many of the features of a theatre performance and, as in the theatre, effective presentation in the courtroom requires sensitive adaptation to the particular circumstances and audience. After watching these barristers at work, some good and some appalling, I decided at that early stage that in a criminal trial, it was necessary that a proffered view was consistent not only with all the objectively demonstrable facts but also with the view that could reasonably be expected to be taken by a jury of the personalities and possible behaviours of those involved. A proposition presented for consideration, whether by a judge or jury, must possess inherent credibility at multiple levels. This represents the difference between a defence which must be psychologically viable and a story that could well accommodate the established facts and still be rejected.

Juries are selected at random from ordinary members of the community. They enter the courtroom with a wide range of experiences and backgrounds, and are required almost every day to assess the likely truthfulness and motivations of the people they encounter. In their normal social interactions, they draw conclusions about what has probably happened in a range of situations relevant—sometimes of crucial importance— to their lives. This ability to sense falsity, and the insights and experience which are necessary in order to function in our complex society, provide the principal justifications for retaining this method of trial and should never be underestimated.

Despite our much-increased knowledge and understandings, we still depend on human experience and perceptions to fill in the blanks. I have great respect for the capacity of most people, when properly informed, to do that. I always proceeded on the assumption that jury members would be alert to my specific objectives and tactics. This was no disadvantage as I regarded it as essential for them to understand and follow the line of argument being presented if ultimately they were to be asked to consider it. Seldom did a jury verdict surprise me, and rarely did I think it was clearly wrong. But, even then, I had to accept that any perceived misjudgement may not have been theirs.

Apart from study, my major involvements throughout this period related to the current social and industrial issues. I had no interest in university student politics and regarded the various clubs as vehicles for self-promotion by extremely ambitious would-be politicians, most of whom I disliked as poseurs. Some later became highly successful and well-respected poseurs, but whether they ever matured beyond their youthful ambitions or had any higher motivation than personal advancement has always been a matter of doubt in my mind. I did not want to engage in what I regarded as meaningless self-indulgent discussions and meetings in a protected university environment where the primary objective seemed to be their individual success, when the real struggles were occurring outside.

The only social activity in which I regularly engaged while at university was track and road bike racing with the local Glenroy club. We used to race on a compacted sand surface that caused extensive gravel rash if you fell, which I did several times. I also participated from time to time in boxing training and bouts in a backyard gym that a waterside worker friend of my father, Joe Laherty, had set up to provide some activity for the district's young men.

In the last of these fights, which were rough and usually more enthusiastic than skilful, I had an opponent who had fought on a popular television program *TV Ringside* and was regarded as 'quite handy'. Unsurprisingly, these contests attracted the attention of some of the local girls who came to watch. My opponent decided to demonstrate his prowess to impress them, and a serious fight developed in which I broke his nose. Rather than risk a return bout, I decided it was time to retire.

POLITICS

Much of my non-study time was occupied with political and industrial issues. These included the reestablishment of the local Australian Labor Party branch. A party split in 1955 had led to the creation of a new organisation, the Democratic Labor Party, and the break-up of many branches. We started with the minimum number of ten members required under the rules. My father was the president, and I became the eighteen-year-old secretary.

I continued to assist my father with the reading and preparation of written material concerning a range of political and industrial issues, as I had been doing in Launceston. He was well known as a union activist and, shortly after our return from Tasmania, became a member of the executive of the Melbourne branch of the union. Consistent with his general perspective, he had no difficulty in cooperating with communists to achieve better pay and improve social conditions for the less well-off in our society; he had been elected on a 'unity ticket' of communists and left-leaning ALP members like himself. I met and understood what motivated these men and was not troubled by either his or my association with them.

The political struggle with the DLP was quite intense and, much to my mother's annoyance, my father was attacked several times in a widely watched television program presented by the National Civic Council, a conservative Catholic lobby group associated with the DLP. This infuriated my mother who stopped going to church for a while after he was criticised from the pulpit.

There were no playgrounds or support services for the large population of young people in the Housing Commission area, so with Kate Laherty, Joe's wife and an effective social organiser, we established a tenants' association to advocate for the residents. My role was primarily to represent the group publicly and to endeavour to secure the necessary political support for the funding and structures required. This was difficult, as the Broadmeadows Council was constituted by local home owners and businessmen who were not at all happy about the creation of the new Housing Commission estate or the people who lived there, while the area held little interest for the major political parties. As an ALP stronghold, the Party was much more concerned to improve its position in less secure electorates and, for the same reason, it held little interest for their opponents. Nevertheless, we were able to secure some small improvements.

It was during this time that my political activities were first mentioned in a newspaper. When it was announced that the State Liberal Party leader, Henry Bolte, would be at a campaign meeting in the electorate, I decided to attend and challenge him. Positioning myself close to the stage, I continually interjected as he was speaking. Eventually he said, 'Young man, you seem to have some strong opinions; why don't you come up here and give us the benefit of them.' That was a bad mistake, as he quickly discovered. When asked to leave, I pointed out that he had invited me to speak and now seemed unable to respond adequately to what I had to say. I thoroughly enjoyed the whole episode. Next morning, one of the newspapers reported the meeting had been disrupted by a 'gang of young hooligans'.

The defection of many ALP members to the rival DLP consequent to the split created difficulty in covering polling booths on election days, and there were concerns about the possibility of violent confrontations as emotions were high on both sides. Equipped with little knowledge of the relevant law and no experience whatever in dealing with issues of that kind, I was sent on one election day to Richmond Town Hall in one of the inner suburbs where trouble was anticipated; I was to assist if any charges were laid against our volunteers in the event of fights breaking out. My father's union provided me with a 'minder', a large and fearsome-looking but good-natured former heavyweight boxer. Possibly because of his intimidating appearance and the fact that he was well known in the area, no difficulty was encountered.

One connection that I particularly enjoyed was with a small and now long defunct trade union, the Federated Marine Stewards and Pantrymen's Association of Australasia. The members were seamen working in catering on passenger and cargo vessels. They were a great group. I was in my second year at university when I attended my first Victorian State Conference of the ALP in 1956 as their delegate, and continued in that role for the next ten years. Except for issues directly involving the members, the union gave me total discretion regarding the vote to be cast, and in that capacity I was able to engage in the debate and vote for the abandonment of the White Australia policy.

It was at the first of these conferences that I was asked to represent an elderly stalwart of the Labor movement named Muriel Heagney. She had come into conflict with other members of the Women's Central Organising Committee of the Party and been removed from her position. Muriel was an amazing person, a pioneer for women's rights who had been involved in radical politics from the early 1900s. She was strong-minded and struggled with the reluctance of both the political party and the male-dominated trade union movement to honour its rhetoric and push for full equality, in particular for equal pay, for women. She strongly disapproved of what she viewed as the 'tea and cakes' approach of the other women' s committee members who she saw as simply supporting the men in a semi-domestic fashion, and she was frequently in conflict with them for their seeming lack of preparedness to advocate for women's rights. In many respects, Muriel was cast in the same mould as Jenny Baines.

Unable to secure a senior member of the Party to represent her in her appeal, Muriel approached another law student, Bill Aughterson, and myself. We succeeded on the conference floor and she was reinstated, but I learned success often comes at a cost. After the vote, as I was leaving the hall, rather pleased with the outcome, one of the consequentially irate committee members, who had apparently moved on from 'tea and cakes', hit me hard across the head and quickly removed any sense of triumph.

NATIONAL SERVICE

Towards the end of my final year, a member of my ALP branch took me to the home of the former Victorian Attorney General, William Slater, who was the senior partner of the legal firm of Slater and Gordon where I hoped to obtain articles of clerkship. This involved twelve months of practical training in a solicitor's office after completion of the degree course and was required before admission to practice. I was accepted and commenced in February 1959 after completing my last national service camp.

Under the scheme then in place, all eighteen-year-old males were required to register for military training. An initial three months had to be served, followed by further camps at the end of each year for the next three years. After completion, they would be liable for reserve call-up for several additional years. I had undergone my training in the army.

My military career could not be described as particularly successful or noteworthy. Although never charged for any of them, I was paraded several times before the regimental sergeant major for various disciplinary infringements. By the time I was required to serve, the Korean War ceasefire had come into effect and, because national service was being abolished, it was clear that mine would be one of the last intakes. In that situation, I found it difficult to take the training and military discipline seriously—luckily a view shared by the sergeant major.

I was stationed at the Watsonia Military Camp in 1956, which was located on the outskirts of the city, when an industrial dispute involving my father's union resulted in waterside workers refusing to load or unload ships in Melbourne. A major area of contention related to a Commonwealth Government plan to establish a new body, the Australian Stevedoring Industry Authority, that would have the power to compel attendance and the provision of answers at hearings on matters affecting the industry. The proposed legislation was clearly directed to reducing the power of the union.

This was met with considerable resistance and a national strike by the waterside workers. The Government responded by threatening to declare a state of emergency and to use troops to load and unload vessels. It was an extraordinary escalation of an industrial dispute. I was concerned that the battalion stationed at Watsonia could become involved in some way.

There was no question in my mind concerning where I stood on this issue. Not only did I have a profound objection in principle to the use of compulsory powers of interrogation to break a union for political purposes, but could not participate as a strike breaker against my father and his fellow workers. This view was also held by a small group of other left-wing student activists who were in camp with me. We decided that we would not only refuse to comply with any orders directed to that objective but also urge our fellow soldiers to stand with us. It was a serious decision that could have resulted in imprisonment and ended my not yet started career in the law. Fortunately, the dispute was resolved and I never needed to go through with it.

I have no doubt that the potential abuse of power and injustice arising from the kinds of measures contemplated at the time of the referendum concerning the Communist Party and this attempt to control union activism have impacted heavily on my view of the importance of adherence to the values inherent in the rule of law. These were reflected in my later work.

AN ARTICLED CLERK

When I commenced my articles, Slater and Gordon was a small firm with four partners. The clients were mostly members of left-wing unions, and the firm was generally regarded with intense disfavour by the conservative legal establishment. My duties were centred around the industrial accident and workers compensation claims that constituted the bulk of the work under the general direction of my principal, Geoff Jones, and another of the partners, Jim Hill, whose brother Ted was a senior figure in the Communist Party of Australia. Ted Hill was an extremely capable barrister with whom I worked on many cases over the years, and I was fond of Jim, who was a wonderful mentor. Slater and Gordon's offices were located in the centre of the city close to the courts and the various barristers' chambers. I would have coffee with Jim most mornings in a coffee lounge on the ground floor of our building with some of the great advocates of the day.

My first day as an articled clerk was memorable in more than one respect. After being taken to my 'office'—a table in the small photocopy room that reeked of the terrible-smelling ink used—I was sent to assist counsel in the High Court in what was known as the Hursey Case. The dispute concerned the power of the Hobart branch of the Waterside Workers' Federation to levy its members to support the ALP. Naturally we represented the union. Among our opponents were John Young, later Chief Justice of Victoria, and John Kerr, whose subsequent controversial role in the dismissal of the Whitlam Labor Government changed the political environment in Australia for many years.

The Hurseys, who were father and son, objected to the levy and sought to have it declared illegal. A similar objection was taken in Victoria, and my father, as a branch official, received a writ claiming several thousand pounds. He was highly amused as there was no possibility that he could have paid anything if they had succeeded. He had it framed and proudly hung it on our lounge room wall.

My delight at being involved in this politically and industrially important case was diminished when it became clear that my primary function was to carry large files to and from the court and to rush about getting books from the library. I went home at the end of the first day with the brand-new suit my parents had bought for me to start work covered in dust from old volumes.

Initially, I was engaged in writing letters, preparing briefs for counsel and organising the attendance of witnesses under the direction of my principal. But soon after I started, I began to handle my own cases and deal directly with clients. Their claims were based generally on injuries or industrial diseases due to their employment in mining or other heavy industry. I liked the work as these were people to whom I could easily relate, and I did my best to help them. I sometimes wonder what they thought about being advised and their cases handled by a twenty-one-year-old, but they would have assumed that I was working under much greater supervision than was the case and no queries were ever raised.

About a month after I started, Geoff Jones sent me to obtain preliminary information from a man hospitalised after sustaining injury. It was a traumatic experience. The fingers of both his hands had been torn off when caught in an unguarded machine. He was deeply distressed following a bedside visit from an insurance investigator, who had suggested to him that his claim could be more quickly handled if he abandoned any attempt to secure civil damages and instead took the much less substantial workers compensation payments that would be immediately available.

When I learned what had happened, I was incensed and immediately rang the insurance company, pointing out (in very blunt language more reminiscent of my waterfront background than professional communication) the potential legal and industrial consequences of such conduct if his weekly payments were not immediately approved. One of their senior officials then called our office a short time later, asserting there must have been some misunderstanding and that there would be no problem.

My principal congratulated me for resolving the issues for our client so quickly, but suggested with some amusement that I need not be as aggressive in future, and to threaten a state-wide industrial stoppage of all union-covered enterprises insured by the company was hardly a lawyer's response. From my perspective, however, this would have been expected if the worker had been a member of my father's union and seemed entirely reasonable, even if I did have no idea how I could follow through on my threat.

One group I encountered in this work and for whom I had high regard were the coalminers from Wonthaggi, a small township in the east of the State. They worked in terrible conditions deep underground, digging out small seams along passages in which they could barely stand. I went into those mines only a couple of times and wondered how the men managed to tolerate being there for full shifts.

An incident that epitomised these mining families occurred some years later when I was briefed as a barrister to act for one of them who was dying of industrial lung disease in his claim for worker's compensation. He arrived early at my room in Owen Dixon Chambers and said that his wife would be joining him. He had come ahead to speak to me as he did not want her to know how bad his condition was. He was worried about how she would cope financially after his death and pressed upon me the importance of doing my best to secure some compensation money for her, emphasising that I was not to be concerned about him. I gave him that undertaking.

After her arrival, we discussed his case and they left. A few minutes later, my client's wife returned: she had deliberately left her handbag under a chair. She wanted me to assure her that under no circumstances was her husband to be subjected to increased stress as a result of the claim. She said that he did not appreciate how fragile his state was. She was aware he wanted to secure some provision for her, but wanted me to understand that the money did not matter. I gave that undertaking also and wondered how I could honour both. In the event, his claim was strong, and we were able to secure what was a reasonable settlement in terms of entitlements under the *Workers Compensation Act*.

The relatively small-scale black coal mining operations conducted in Victoria in which these men worked were coming to an end and little was done to mechanise them, so pit ponies were used in these mines until they ceased in the late 1960s. One of my early cases involved them. They were small, strong animals that dragged the heavy skips of coal along a narrow railway from the work faces. At the end of their shifts, the ponies were released into the mine paddocks. As soon as the gate was opened, they would rush to the light and open air. On this occasion, the worker ordinarily responsible for their welfare was on leave and his temporary replacement was standing in the wrong position. In consequence, he was crushed between the gate and a fence as they surged forward.

Horses were also still used on the wharves to move cargo between the ships and the storage sheds until the late 1950s and were the subject of one of the industrial stoppages in which my father was involved. After a long dispute, the union had succeeded in its campaign to abolish extended shifts. These were used by stevedoring companies to minimise the costs when loading was nearing completion. A major problem from the workers' perspective was that the risk of injury increased substantially due to tiredness and reduced concentration with the increased hours. When it was discovered at a change of shift that this limitation did not extend to the horses, the workers went on strike. They argued that, if men had to work like horses, horses should not have to work longer than men. Success for the horses proved considerably easier to achieve.

My friend, Barney Cooney, was articled in another city firm, and he used to make some extra money serving process for them after hours. I sometimes accompanied him. On one of these occasions, we served an eviction notice on some unfortunate people in a slum property in one of our poorest areas. The sad-looking woman who answered the door started to cry, and it was too much for us. We spent the next hour advising the family on how to deal with the situation.

There was much to learn about the practice of the law, as I quickly discovered. Shortly after I started, I was assigned to assist in a case where we were acting as the Victorian agent of a Sydney legal firm in a Supreme Court civil action. The opposition had secured an order for the production of relevant documents, and cartons containing thousands of them arrived at the office. It didn't occur to me that they had been delivered unsorted, and at the last moment before the hearing, to limit the possibility of analysis. I worked late into the night organising them. However, my well-intentioned endeavours to assist everyone were not appreciated by the clients, as they resulted in the almost instant exposure of the serious problems in their position. As soon as they saw the plaintiff's lawyers going through the carefully arranged documents, they left the court and caught the next plane back to Sydney. Our case immediately collapsed.

A barrister I briefed during my time as an articled clerk, and with whom I subsequently developed a strong relationship, was Edward (Ted) Laurie. In one matter, we represented the plaintiff in what must have been one, if not the last, of the final breach of promise of marriage actions argued in Australia. It was a bizarre cause of action, reflective of another age when female 'virtue' was regarded as having an economic value. Our client claimed that she had engaged in sex with the defendant on the assurance they would be married. Unwilling to honour this promise, he had sought advice from his solicitors which they provided in a letter that came into our client's possession. It read: 'If you do not wish to marry the above-mentioned woman, we suggest that you engage in delicate procrastination'. By the 1960s, however, a claim of this kind for damages was not taken seriously, and we lost.

I developed enormous respect for Ted as a lawyer and, much more importantly, as a kind and generous person. He was one of the intellectuals of his era who saw in communism a solution to the systemic problems that had led to the Great Depression of the 1930s and the related rise of Nazism and Fascism. He was concerned with human values and the plight of the poor and the exploited. By the time I met him, although this commitment had not lessened, he no longer saw the answers to social injustices in the kinds of authoritarian structures or policies represented by the communist states or the doctrinaire application of Marxist theory. At the end of that year, he 'moved' my admission to practise.

A few years later, when Ted applied for appointment as Queen's Counsel, the politically conservative and deeply prejudiced Chief Justice, Sir Edmund Herring, refused to recommend him. He also refused to endorse the first woman to apply. It is indicative of the respect in which both were held within the legal profession, on his retirement, that they were immediately endorsed by his successor and appointed.

SOLICITOR

In some important ways, my situation improved substantially during this year. I was happy in my work, continued my political involvements and began to meet up with other young lawyers who were undertaking their articles in nearby firms. Until a few years earlier, articled clerks who had completed their degree courses were not only unpaid, but also required to give their principal fifty guineas (a guinea was one pound and one shilling) for their training. By the standards of the time I was well off, receiving ten pounds per week. The general rate was between six and eight pounds. At that stage, I had not considered going to the bar and was anticipating a career as a solicitor.

Although I was involved in various political activities, I was not interested in pursuing a career in that area. My extensive exposure from an early age to the manoeuvres and blatant unprincipled opportunism of many of those seeking to secure or retain office constituted a powerful discouragement. I had watched deeply committed people cynically taken advantage of time after time. My father, who was certainly not naive, was well aware of the venality of many, if not most, of those involved. But he was concerned with the potential outcomes and the necessity to continue the struggle to achieve a fair and decent society, and persisted. Although there were fortunately some wonderful individuals to whom my description did not apply, I knew that I would never be comfortable with the factional commitment, manoeuvring and personal compromises required to succeed in that environment. There was too much in political party operations that resembled George Orwell's *Animal Farm*.

I enjoyed my year at Slater and Gordon but the partners had not given any indication I could remain, so when Clyde Holding offered to employ me, I accepted. It is doubtful that the partners would have been troubled had I gone to any other firm, but Holding was a direct and ambitious competitor for union work. The partners never completely shunned me at the bar as a consequence of my decision, but they were obviously annoyed, and briefed me only occasionally until I had independently established myself, some eight years later.

As I mentioned earlier, it was on my first day at work for Holding that I met Dawn. She thought I was far too self-impressed and, in more than one respect—and certainly from her viewpoint—this was a reasonable assessment. I wanted to impress this beautiful girl and felt delighted with my new position as a solicitor and the fact I was now receiving twenty pounds a week.

My work remained essentially the same, with one significant difference: I began to make appearances in procedural applications before courts and in small civil and criminal cases in the Magistrates Court, then called the Court of Petty Sessions. There were plenty of opportunities for this.

At that time, judges and magistrates often treated inexperienced young practitioners badly. Bullying was common and seemed to be regarded as a necessary rite of passage that would equip the young person for work in an environment of conflict and disputation.

One experience of this kind that left me extremely angry involved a claim for workers compensation by a Commonwealth employee. On the second day of the hearing, I arrived about twenty minutes before the court was due to resume and found that the barrister I had briefed was not there. No one had told me he had arranged to have the case stood down until the afternoon. Unable to contact him, when the judge came onto the bench to make the formal order, I requested a short adjournment to locate him.

Apparently having nothing better to do, the judge decided to amuse himself at my expense. He said nothing about the arrangement and refused, disingenuously pointing out that the major medical witness for the Commonwealth was available for cross-examination and he would probably have to excuse him. In that situation, he said the witness's evidence would stand unchallenged. With no idea what to do and concerned about the impact this might have on the client's case, I decided that I would have to try to stall until the barrister arrived. The judge then said that, if this was my intention, it would not work, because under the rules governing barristers' conduct, he would be regarded as dismissed from the case.

He then asked me, 'Well, what are you going to do now?' Being completely out of my depth, I felt I had no choice but to go ahead. 'Good boy,' he said and, having decided the game had been played out, adjourned.

BACK TO PORT MELBOURNE

My first criminal case was argued, without fee, in the Court of Petty Sessions at Port Melbourne about three months after I was admitted to practice and only two blocks from my early home in Graham Street. The client was an unemployed Maori man charged with receiving stolen property of small value. Although the magistrate needed little persuasion to release him without conviction, I returned to my office feeling triumphant.

Coincidentally, my last appearance before going onto the bench was also without fee and before a magistrate on behalf of a woman charged with receiving stolen property. My client on that occasion was the relative of a friend. The thief had stolen some chairs and a table from a holiday home and had given them to the friend to furnish her Housing Commission flat. The result was the same. I had hoped to finish my time as a barrister with a greater flourish, but it seemed appropriate that the wheel had turned full circle.

I was at the Port Melbourne courthouse a few weeks after this first appearance when I heard a voice call, 'Frankie, Frankie!' On looking around, I saw one of my cousins waving to attract my attention from the cell block. He had contracted cerebral meningitis when young and sustained permanent brain damage. Although he was much older than Brian and me, when we were children we saw and interacted with him as a big kid.

Court officials informed me that he was charged with assault and resisting arrest by a police member who, it seems, had reacted to his unusual presentation and taken hold of him. Not understanding, and frightened by what was happening, my cousin had tried to break away and was then overpowered.

There was no doubt in my mind that once the magistrate understood the situation, the charges would be dismissed. Rather than attempting to provide an explanation without any supporting material, I decided it should be sufficient for my unfortunate cousin to give evidence.

'Would you please state your name?' I asked.

'You know me, Frankie.'

'Of course, but you have to tell this man.'

After a few more questions, the magistrate indicated he had heard enough and severely criticised all of the police involved in the process for their unnecessary heavy-handed treatment of a person with a severe disability.

I liked this appearance work, almost all of which was undertaken on a *pro bono* basis, and took every opportunity that emerged over the months that followed. The cases were generally concerned with minor criminal offences, claims for maintenance by deserted wives and unmarried mothers, and defences to debt recovery processes.

At lunch one day after I had been working at Holding Ryan and Co. for a little over a year, Barney Cooney told me he had decided to go to the bar and suggested I should consider joining him. This was an attractive idea, as I had begun to feel I was better suited to that role.

When the possibility was raised with Holding, he said that because of the nature of the cases undertaken by the firm, they were unlikely to be able to give me much support until I had gained substantially more experience. He indicated that I would need to remain with the firm for at least another two years. That seemed an interminable time to wait, so I gave notice.

I realised that I would almost certainly be without any income for several months and, having no savings or other financial support, was taking a huge gamble. However, I was still living at home with my parents and reasoned that I should be able to keep my expenses to a minimum until I could establish myself. Fortunately, the then President of the Melbourne branch of the Waterside Workers' Federation, Jim Cummins, came to my rescue and loaned me one hundred pounds. While this represented only one month's income, it was just enough. He had been elected on a right-wing group ticket and was a member of the Democratic Labor Party. My father and he were opposed politically, but I was the son of a fellow wharf labourer and had the chance to go to the bar. That loyalty was regarded as far more significant.

About a week before leaving, I gained the courage to ask Dawn to go out with me. We were in a courtroom where a client's claim for damages was proceeding when I passed a note to her suggesting that we go to the Shirley Bassey show. (She was an internationally successful popular singer who was coming to Melbourne on tour).

After expressing initial uncertainty about whether I was serious, Dawn agreed. After the show, we talked for a long time before I took her home. It seemed easy and natural. So began a love affair that has now lasted for more than a half-century.

THE BAR

I signed the role of counsel on 5 March 1961 and commenced 'reading' with Ted Laurie. There was no induction or training system for new barristers (it was many years before one was introduced) but they were required to remain for six months in the chambers of an experienced member who would act as a mentor or 'master'.

When I approached Ted, he advised me that, given his well-known political involvements, association with him would almost certainly be damaging to my career prospects. While I recognised the force of his warning, I was not troubled by the thought that I would be viewed unfavourably by many within the largely conservative legal profession. I did not anticipate their support in any event and I never wanted to conceal my background or views.

Upon any reasonable assessment, it was an inauspicious beginning. Not only did I have almost no money, no helpful social connections and no reliable source of work in the profession, but I had also chosen to read in the chambers of a senior and—in the eyes of many—notorious communist, in the depths of the period of hostility between the Soviet bloc and the Western powers known as the Cold War. I certainly do not regret this decision and have always been proud of my connection with this kind and principled teacher.

It was also necessary to join the list of one of the three clerks approved by the Bar Council. A barrister's clerk sends out accounts, negotiates and collects fees and attends to booking arrangements for those on their list. They were paid through the inclusion of a small fee for each brief. Importantly from my perspective, the clerk provided a major point of contact for solicitors seeking suitable counsel for their cases, and I was hopeful I would get some exposure and work this way. Again, I was very fortunate in being accepted by a clerk who had enough confidence in me to put my name forward for consideration.

For a long time, Ted's prediction proved correct, and there were many solicitors who throughout my entire time at the bar would never have been prepared to brief me, even if I were the best qualified or the last counsel available. The State Crown Solicitor was a substantial source of work for the junior members who was also unavailable to me because of my political associations and relationship with him. There was little prospect of securing work from any of the larger well-established firms, and in any event, I had no contacts to call on in any of them. I knew I could expect little support from Holding, and the partners at Slater and Gordon were unhappy that I had left to work for him.

A further problem was created by the introduction of a 'credit squeeze' by the Commonwealth Government that reduced the availability of low-level 'floating' briefs for the junior bar. Many more of the smaller cases were either not contested or handled by the local solicitors themselves. Nevertheless, immunised by the totally unjustified confidence of youth, these practical considerations were regarded as relatively insignificant impediments along my path.

My first brief, which was secured through my clerk, was to cross-examine an Italian man in a debt recovery process in the County Court concerning his failure to pay the amount outstanding under a contract with a company that had financed his family's migration to Australia. The unfortunate individuals who entered these exploitative arrangements in the expectation of earning substantial incomes in their new country often found themselves with huge interest obligations they could not meet. The Court officer dealing with the case was singularly unimpressed by my arguments concerning the justice of my client's position and dismissed the claim. I would have liked to start with a more deserving cause.

Preparations for occupancy of new premises to house the bar had not yet been completed and most members were still located in an old and unsatisfactory building near the courts. The rooms were small and located on each side of a central corridor, which extended for the entire length of the building and opened into the next street. Readers would commonly need to confer with their clients on benches in the middle of this passage as barristers, solicitors and members of the public passed by.

The Victorian Bar had about two hundred practising members at that time, and I soon became acquainted with almost all of them. This was assisted by a convention that applied when we moved to a new building about three months after I started called Owen Dixon Chambers, under which it was considered impolite not to take the next available seat at the lunch or coffee table regardless of who was there.

As I had anticipated, much of my work was obtained from suburban practices. These were usually situated near the many local courthouses or halls where hearings in the Court of Petty Sessions were held. Some of these firms were substantial businesses and became good sources for me. The briefs were initially secured through my clerk as 'floaters' in the lower courts. They were usually small cases where, for one reason or another, no counsel was engaged.

I adopted the policy of never refusing or treating this work lightly no matter how minor the case, how small the fee, how much travelling time was involved or even how little I knew about the subject. The last problem, I reasoned, could be solved by research and it was essential to be seen and to make myself known around the courts as a competent barrister. Every case therefore became a test to which I applied myself as if it were being argued in the High Court.

For the first year I had no car, and travelling to and from the various courthouses by train was often time-consuming. The journey from my home in Glenroy to the other side of the city to represent clients of my friend Bill Aughterson—then employed as a first-year solicitor—and then back to chambers in the frequently vain hope that there might be work for the next day, would take hours.

I was eager to see Dawn as much as possible, and we would meet for a short time for coffee after she finished work. At weekends I used to ride my bike the fifteen kilometres to her home. Not surprisingly, her father thought there was something strange about a barrister who was six years older than his teenage daughter, had no car and obviously no money. He also strongly disapproved of my political views and union affiliations.

When I finally did get a car, a small Fiat 1100 cc with a noisy engine that would have powered a sewing machine, life became easier and it became possible to accept briefs from country firms. One round trip of about five hundred kilometres to the north of the State cost my entire fee, but I regarded all exposure and experience as valuable.

I kept that first car until a couple of years after we were married, when Dawn drove it into a tree while I was giving her a driving lesson. It was too badly damaged to be repaired, and I received a nasty head wound and concussion. My attempt to go to court two days later was abandoned when I fell over in the street a few steps from home while walking to the bus stop. Nevertheless, rather than miss out on the fee, I appeared for a client in the County Court within a week with a head bandage instead of a barrister's wig.

Slowly but surely, I began to develop a network of support. As a self-claimed expert in just about everything, I would be briefed by an increasing number of small suburban firms based on their understanding of my areas of practice. Although it was not seen as more than necessary for survival at the time, engaging in such a wide range of cases was good training. Most of the firms had only a small amount of litigation, but collectively they enabled me to keep going. I am extremely grateful for the support and the confidence in me that these solicitors demonstrated—some of them over many years.

One of the solicitors who briefed me in the early days was a well-known criminal lawyer, Ray Dunn. He would hand off work that he was too busy to handle himself in the suburban courts to junior bar members. Through Ray, I met his articled clerk, John Coldrey, who became and has remained a close friend. John is a highly intelligent, principled person, and we worked together in various roles for many years, including trials in Victoria and with Aboriginal communities in the Northern Territory. John was later appointed Victoria's Director of Public Prosecutions and then a judge of the Supreme Court. Having few in the legal profession to advance our interests, John and I agreed to take every opportunity to mention each other; we still do.

There were, of course, no mobile phones or internet at that time, and having no substantial practice I would wait in my room from eight-thirty in the morning when the clerk's office opened until five-thirty in the afternoon when it closed, hoping the phone would ring with an offer of work. The longest period that it remained silent while I sat waiting was three weeks. That was a dreadful time as both my money and confidence slowly ebbed away. I had secured a small bank overdraft and often approached the limit, but there was always just enough work to enable me to keep going and I was determined to persist while I could. Not to succeed was regarded as bad enough, but I would have been ashamed of myself if I had given up while there remained any chance at all. That would have represented real failure.

For a while after finishing my reading period, I shared a room with another barrister, Fred James, who had signed the bar role at the same time. This was an unusual arrangement, but the senior members responsible for accommodation were very helpful, recognising that rent was an issue for us.

Fred was in a similar financial position, and we encouraged each other. His father had also worked on the waterfront for a short time before enlisting in the army. Following his death from war injuries, Fred, who was remarkably gifted, had been assisted through his studies by a Legacy scholarship as a child of a deceased soldier. He was determined to succeed but like me had few contacts in a tightly knit legal community where family and social connections were of substantial assistance in getting started. We came to know each other well as we sat by our telephones. Perhaps the most saddening characteristic of my friend was the extent to which he genuinely underestimated his abilities. This made him a rarity among the self-impressed young males who comprised our contemporaries, but ultimately it held him back and denied him the recognition and level of success to which he was entitled. Fred died of a heart condition in his early fifties.

Financial survival remained a problem, but there was another dimension to my early years at the bar. I generally enjoyed the work and was pleased with my developing skills and the camaraderie that developed in a small group of new members, including Fred and Barney. None of us had a complete set of robes, so we shared two that were kept in a locker in the Supreme Court building across the road from barristers' chambers. As we seldom required them, this did not present a problem until the day when, inevitably, I found they were being used. The judge before whom I was to appear was exceedingly stern-looking and a stickler for protocol. In answer to his query about why he should permit me to appear before him 'unrobed', I told him I was last to the locker and that the set I shared with some other young counsel had gone. He sat silent for what seemed an interminable time, then smiling broadly said, 'That could *only* be true.' Contrary to his intimidating reputation and probably as a result, I always found him pleasant to appear before.

One day I received a call from my clerk, who told me that Victoria's most prominent criminal law solicitor, Frank Galbally, wanted someone to represent a client charged with a minor theft offence at a Court of Petty Sessions on the following morning. I would happily have accepted a brief for any day in any court in the foreseeable future and told the clerk to let him know that I was available. When my phone then rang, Galbally, who I had never met and who knew nothing of me, said in what I soon learned was his typical showman style how delighted he was that someone of my recognised brilliance as a young barrister could appear for his client. The case went well, and he began to provide me with work.

To hand off smaller cases in this way was common practice among the solicitors operating in the criminal courts. Another of the young barristers arrived at a court one morning to meet his client for the first time. The client, who had expected the solicitor, was singularly unimpressed and rejected him, saying, 'I did not buy a first-class ticket to travel in a third-class carriage'.

Ted Laurie was helpful during this early period and provided me with 'devilling' work. Busy senior barristers would sometimes engage young members to conduct research and draft documents for them. I paid for Dawn's engagement ring, and we saved for our honeymoon with money earned in this way. We would go to Ted's room on Saturdays and Sundays, and I would prepare material while she typed the drafts. Although this activity may not appear to have been particularly romantic, we enjoyed preparing for our life together.

We were married in July 1963. Neither Dawn's parents nor mine were happy about this at first. Apart from the fact that they understandably considered Dawn too young and thought we should have waited, her parents, who had experienced family conflict because of their own 'mixed' marriage, were upset because she was marrying into a Catholic family, and mine because I wasn't. However, the situation settled down, and the ceremony was held in the Independent Church in central Melbourne, which was chosen solely because of its name. We later resolved the issue of our children's religious affiliations by not requiring them to have any.

Dawn had also left Holding, Ryan and Co. by that time, and after initially working for a company that operated cattle stations, she started with another firm of solicitors. Her wage provided our only reliable income and enabled us to rent a particularly nice flat in Elwood. Although I concealed it from everyone except her, the fact that I was making little progress began to erode my confidence. I had decided that, once my overdraft limit was reached, I would regard my attempt as unsuccessful and look for a job as a solicitor. Several times we were within a few dollars of it but Dawn was wonderfully strong, never once expressing any concern about the situation, although, as she told me much later, it was a very stressful time for her.

My father assumed I had been instantly successful, and he would call me almost daily to inquire about what I was doing. Rather than disappoint him with the truth, which often was that I hadn't had any work for some days, I would tell him of a case I had heard about or watched. He would then proudly relate a fictional string of brilliant successes to his workmates. From my perspective, these calls emphasised my lack of progress and I hated the deception involved. His enthusiasm created a bit of a problem when one of his workmates was charged with a minor traffic offence, and my father asked me to represent him. On arriving at the court, I was dismayed to find not only my client but my father and most of the other workers. The magistrate, who quickly summed up the situation, congratulated me profusely on my presentation and imposed a minimal penalty. My father was delighted.

The only other time he saw me in court was some years later when I was representing the plaintiff in a Supreme Court civil injuries case. An issue arose about the extent of our client's knowledge of his legal rights. In the course of cross-examination, he said he had spoken to a union official, named Frank Vincent, about his case. The defendant's barrister thought he might be able to use this connection to his advantage. When the hearing resumed after lunch, my father's name was called and he came into the court. He had been shovelling coal when a subpoena had been served upon him, and entered covered in black dust and carrying his sweat-stained work hat. Shrewdly, he had decided not to change his clothes or wash. When he saw me at the bar table, he smiled broadly and said, 'Hello, son.' I responded, 'G'day, Dad.' It was a magical moment, which the subsequent amount of damages awarded to our client suggests was not lost on the jury. The conversation had taken place in a hotel bar after work one evening, and the injured man was certainly not relying upon my father's legal expertise.

CRIME

My first criminal trial brief was given to me as a 'floater' by the Public Solicitor at the last minute after the accused had insisted on proceeding. His defence was clearly viewed as hopeless and it was anticipated he would plead guilty. He, however, had a very different perspective on being charged with causing grievous bodily harm, considering it completely unfair and insisting the man he had savagely beaten had merely received his 'right whack' in the circumstances.

The victim and he were career criminals who had committed factory thefts together. My client, when caught, refused to seek a reduction in sentence by divulging the name of his accomplice. There could be little surprise that he was then infuriated when, during his time in prison, his companion ungraciously not only spent the proceeds of their activities but also sold the belongings that had been left with him for safekeeping. From my client's viewpoint, this was an appalling breach of trust that merited, at minimum, a severe beating, and he did not accept he had done anything more than respond appropriately. He was confident the jury would understand the justice of his position and acquit him.

This appreciation of the situation was not shared by the trial judge, who became more and more annoyed by my obvious inexperience as I clumsily endeavoured to explore the relationship between the two men and present his perspective. He correctly regarded the nature of their prior involvement as providing no lawful justification whatsoever for the accused's behaviour and repeatedly criticised my efforts in front of the jury.

As might be expected, the trial was a disaster until finally the client intervened. He said to the judge, 'Give the kid a chance. You can see he's not done much of this sort of thing, but he's having a proper go for me and he's not bad. You and this guy [pointing to the prosecutor] are running in harness. He shouldn't have to fight both of you, and I'm the one who will have the gate shut on him.'

Horrified, I slumped into my seat.

The jury retired shortly afterwards and quickly returned a verdict of not guilty. Whether they accepted the justice of my client's position as he anticipated, or were concerned about the fairness of his trial, I don't know, but I had my result. My briefing solicitor, who had not been present for what he presumably anticipated would be a debacle, was most impressed. I decided I need not trouble him with the details of what had transpired, accepting his surprised congratulations with appropriate humility.

Three years after I signed the roll, Bill Aughterson sent me my first brief to defend a person charged with murder. By that time, I had represented clients in only a handful of substantial criminal cases, none of which would have suggested to an observer that I could sensibly be entrusted with this responsibility. I told my client—a twenty-six-year-old petty criminal who bore the appropriate nickname 'Lard Head' among his associates—that I had never handled a case approaching that level of seriousness, and suggested he should have someone with much more experience appear for him. He said he was not concerned and that it was a first for him, too.

The circumstances were broadly similar to those in a previous case in Victoria only twelve years earlier, which had resulted in three offenders being executed, one of them the last female to suffer the death penalty. Similarly, my client was one of a group of three that the prosecution alleged had been involved in the torture and killing of a victim while in the process of robbing him. Here, the victim was an elderly pensioner, who they wrongly believed had money hidden in his bungalow. My client was keeping watch while the others tried to force the man to disclose where he had concealed it. The similarities suggested that, if convicted, there was a distinct possibility that 'Lard Head' could be hanged or, at least, spend most of the rest of his life in prison.

While the sentence of death by hanging was formally imposed on all convictions of adult offenders, by the 1960s it was almost always commuted, and the term of imprisonment fixed by the Governor in Council that allowed for the offender's eventual consideration for release on parole. I was acutely aware that only two years previously, the State Government had been prevented by the High Court from proceeding with an execution because of the offender's mental state. The last hanging in Victoria would be carried out just three years later.

Preparing my final address to the jury was one of the most nerve-wracking experiences of my time as a barrister. I was conscious of the enormous responsibility involved and my lack of experience when the outcome of the trial could have been the death of a stupid young man. However, when I finally stood to commence, my performance anxiety dissipated. Relying on the stage presence developed through my earlier training performing in Tasmania, I stepped into the role and presented my arguments without reference to the notes I had laboriously prepared. Almost without conscious thought, I began to adjust my emphases to sensed jury responses, thereby setting a pattern from which I never later departed.

*

More generally, as I gained experience in subsequent trials, I employed a number of techniques to deal with sources of nervousness and create the best possible image for the jury. Obviously, it was necessary to prepare thoroughly, but there were other minor things that were of assistance. Among them was my purchase of two sets of court clothing that were always kept freshly laundered. I would change completely before every final address. I was careful to avoid any casual interaction with others involved in the trial that might be observed by jury members or engage in banter at the bar table. There could be nothing detracted from the appearance of total commitment to my client's case.

Over time, I developed a process that involved carefully structuring my argument on a sequence of propositions and supporting evidence that I prepared in my head and then presenting them unscripted and without reference to notes. Provided that I had developed a clear framework, it was possible to incorporate changes as required. This approach allowed substantial opportunity for structured spontaneity and flexibility in my presentation and continuing adaptation of emphasis and argument to perceived jury responses. I had taken up long-distance running, and I would formulate and silently rehearse what I proposed to say during my nightly training sessions.

I have always been surprised by the limited understanding that many barristers seem to have of the art and techniques of successful communication and strove to improve my own skills, practising in front of a mirror and recording myself reading passages from novels and poems. This was particularly important when referring to written materials. They would also be positioned in advance on the bar table to avoid a break in the flow of my argument and possible severance of my immediate communication link with the jury.

Throughout my time as a barrister, I never ceased to be nervous when appearing in court and, particularly, as I began to present the final address in a criminal trial. Rather than trying to conceal it at that stage, I decided to use it by relating it to my responsibility to ensure that the defence position was before them as clearly and effectively as I could, and to their responsibility to consider it carefully in their endeavour to arrive at a correct verdict.

Although my approach may seem challenging and risky, that was seldom the situation. The outcome in almost all criminal trials depends on the determination of a small number of issues which, if the case is properly prepared, will be identified by a competent lawyer well before a jury is empanelled. Only in the rarest cases should anything unanticipated occur, and normally the delivery of a complete final address should be possible before a single witness gives evidence. I always felt annoyed when barristers claimed they had been unsuccessful because the case had taken a surprising turn or because their client had failed to impress the jury when giving evidence. Usually, the failure was theirs.

The major problem with my technique was that it required immense concentration at all stages of the preparation and conduct of the defence, and was mentally and emotionally demanding. Sometimes, although my objectives were clear, I would not identify the most effective way of introducing evidence or cross-examining a witness until almost the last minute as I gauged the atmosphere in the courtroom and gained a sense of the witness. The answer was sometimes found in the expressions they employed,words chosen or missing that pointed to areas of sensitivity in their narratives and from which they wanted to deflect attention or employed to create a particular impression. I tried to gain an intuitive sense of what I could best describe as the colour of their language. Often, by the end of a trial, I would be exhausted by the effort and tension involved.

*

In that first murder trial, I had decided it would be necessary to finish my address to the jury with a statement that would resonate in their deliberations. After a great deal of thought, I decided upon the formulation: 'It could be that this trial will end with the snap of a gallows rope or the clang of a gaol gate. I pray that it is not in the moment of silence that will follow either of these dreadful sounds that you discover the true meaning of the expression "beyond reasonable doubt", for then it will be too late.'

Afterwards, when the jury retired to consider their verdict, the judge threatened me with possible disciplinary action for this statement which breached a curious rule forbidding counsel to refer to the death penalty. This was based on the idea that the jury should not be concerned with the sentence that may be imposed but only with whether the accused could be properly convicted on the evidence. Reference to the death penalty was seen as irrelevant to their function and as an implied invitation for them to consider it in their deliberations. However, he took no action, nor did any other later judge for what would become my habitual disregard of this restriction. I wanted juries to remain fully aware of the possible consequences of their findings, and the judges had no objection although they were formally obliged to reprimand me.

Waiting for jury verdicts in criminal trials was always stressful, and particularly so in death penalty cases. It was certainly so in that case when they returned at about eleven o'clock on a Friday night. This was not uncommon as jury deliberations could continue late into the night at that time if they indicated that a verdict might be reached. Fortunately, they accepted the defence contention that the evidence was not sufficient for them to find that my client participated in the extreme violence that resulted in the victim's death, and returned a verdict of manslaughter.

One of my saddest visual images of late-night verdicts is of the parents of a victim in another trial holding hands as they walked away from a court at about one-thirty in the morning along a silent, wet street after the conviction of my client who had killed their daughter, their duty performed. Securing justice for a loved one is usually the last thing that can be done for them. Once the legal process is completed, the final link is severed. 'Nothing beside remains' except memories and a void that can never be filled.

In cases involving death or serious injury, rarely can anyone be described as a winner, but there are almost always people who suffer terrible anguish and continuing loss. I have a vivid memory of looking down from the bench at the parents of a young man who had just been convicted of manslaughter arising from his drunken behaviour in a hotel, their hopes and aspirations for him completely shattered. On the other side of the court sat a young mother holding a baby that would never know the father who had been working a second job at the hotel on that night to secure the deposit for a house for them. There was no winner, and nothing anyone could do would restore the situation for those affected. Some people just lose more than others—sometimes much more.

By the time the death penalty was abolished eleven years later, it had become highly unlikely it would be imposed, but the pressure involved in appearing for the defence in such cases was still enormous, and to hear the ritual pronouncement made, as I did on four occasions, was terrible. After that, for the remainder of my time at the bar, the penalty was imprisonment for life without parole, so the stakes were always high.

*

Because of our successful defence in that first trial, it was not long before I received another brief to defend a man charged with murder. The victim was a builder who had a safe in his house which a group of local criminals believed contained money that he kept at home to avoid taxation. They decided to intimidate him into opening it. When he responded to a knock on his front door and saw men outside, he quickly slammed it shut. One of the robbers reacted instinctively, firing the rifle he was carrying. The bullet passed through the door and struck the victim, killing him.

It was clear that my client had been involved in the plan, but there was no evidence that he was aware of the presence of a loaded firearm, and at the time the shot was fired, he was some distance away keeping watch. After negotiation, the prosecution agreed to reduce the murder charge to manslaughter if all members of the group pleaded guilty. The others involved quickly agreed, as they were in much greater jeopardy, and considerable pressure was exerted on my client and myself, but we held out. Finally, the prosecution accepted our offer to plead guilty only to conspiracy to commit robbery, and my client was soon released. It was the best possible result in the circumstances, and from then on, the Public Solicitor came to regard me as someone who could be briefed in homicide cases when more senior counsel were unavailable.

Practice in the criminal law was not generally regarded favourably by the bar, although a few did specialise in this area. No Queen's Counsel were appointed from those who worked exclusively in the criminal courts until the late 1970s, and no Supreme Court judge until 1982. Most of the representation of accused in the Court of Petty Sessions, and some in the County Court and Supreme Court, was handled by solicitors.

Legal aid services were limited and the fees paid to barristers were low. Often in order to secure the services of the few barristers who had developed substantial practices in criminal cases, the defence was funded by Sunday morning backyard functions with barrels of beer. Community and Aboriginal legal aid services were also not established until the mid-1970s and many individuals went before the courts on serious charges without legal assistance.

It was regarded as one of the responsibilities of Queen's Counsel, if available, to accept Public Solicitor murder briefs. While there were some who handled these cases brilliantly, the lack of interest generally in the criminal law, and the ease with which this obligation could be avoided, also resulted in many of the accused in death penalty cases being represented by commercial law specialists with little jury trial experience in either civil or criminal cases. For this reason, once it was accepted that I could handle trials at this level and was prepared to undertake them for the low fees involved, I became identified with the area.

Criminal law issues also held little interest for the Bar Council, which was primarily composed of ambitious individuals practising in more remunerative and 'respectable' areas, and certainly for more socially acceptable clients. I found it ironical that many of this 'nicer' class were little more than corporate bandits who preyed on the public and caused immense social damage. Unease about this disregard began to be expressed when a number of criminal lawyers became involved in the pro bono representation of draft resisters during the Vietnam conflict and then in the development of volunteer-based community legal services. Members of the same group provided the nucleus of support for the establishment of Aboriginal legal services in Victoria and the Northern Territory. After prison riots in 1972, the Victorian State Government established a Commission of Inquiry and, when requests for support for prisoner representation were refused, the group provided the funds to enable one of us to appear for them.

In 1978, four of us established the first splinter group within the bar, the Criminal Bar Association, to advance the interests of those practising in the area, and advocate on a range of legal and social justice issues that became apparent in our work. Criminal lawyers are confronted almost every day with the reality and consequences of social disadvantage in its many manifestations, and the disparity between the publicly asserted values of our society and the actual situations of far too many of its members.

The right to a fair trial at which all of the issues were properly addressed. and the fixing of a sentence based on all of the important considerations and circumstances, should not, in our view, depend on the financial position of the accused; it was the duty of the bar as a professional body with specialist knowledge and insights to advocate to ensure that the rule of law was implemented in our legal system. We decided to run candidates for election to the Bar Council and secured better representation of our perspective. Although our activities were unpopular among senior members, particularly among those eager for judicial appointment and keen to avoid any confrontation with the Government, there was little they could do. Soon, new groups formed in other areas of practice.

*

Fortunately, societal attitudes and consequently some of the work involved in criminal law practice have changed over the years. Engaging in homosexual relations was still treated as criminal at that time, and I acted on behalf of several unfortunate men who found themselves publicly humiliated and at risk of imprisonment when they were entrapped by undercover police members in hotels and toilet blocks. Some subjected themselves to a form of aversion therapy to avoid this outcome. The 'treatment' consisted of the presentation of images designed to induce a sexual response that would be detected by monitoring eye movements, and then associated with the receipt of painful electric shocks. Of course, this could not, and was not intended to, change their underlying orientation, but to modify their behaviour by producing a Pavlovian response of intense distress and nausea if they became sexually aroused. The whole situation was appalling.

Even greater difficulty was encountered when acting for transgender people. One judge was so affronted by the appearance of my client who wore a dress to court and her explanation for engaging in 'male' prostitution—she was trying to make money to travel to

Singapore where it was possible to undergo a gender reassignment procedure—that he spontaneously blurted out, 'It's disgusting.' He imposed a minimal fine to get rid of us.

Drug trafficking, particularly in heroin, had begun to emerge as a problem in the early 1970s, but the judges who dealt with such cases had little understanding of addiction with its physical and psychological consequences. In one case in which I was engaged, the judge refused to delay hearing the plea on sentence, although it was apparent my client, a young woman, was experiencing severe withdrawal symptoms. She had been on bail and using heroin right up to the day of the hearing. After she collapsed in the dock, I sought an adjournment so she could receive assistance. This was refused, and the matter was stood down until the following day, when the process was repeated. By the third day, I was really angry when I found her curled up in a foetal position and dry retching on the floor of the cell behind the court. After the judge took his place on the bench, I carried her into the court and, while still holding her, delivered the plea on her behalf. I then laid her on the bar table and walked out in disgust.

One interesting aspect of the incident is that nothing was ever said to me by the judge or anyone else by way of criticism of my conduct. I assume that what had occurred was the subject of too much embarrassment.

In another drug case, my client was one of several young cannabis users who had investigated the possibility of importing a drum of cannabis oil from Indonesia. The Australian Federal Police had become aware of their discussions and clumsy attempts to find a criminally inclined pilot who would take the obvious risk involved. The individual that the group approached to ascertain if their idea was feasible had informed the police, who arranged for him to provide a quotation that sufficiently lowered the costs for them to go ahead. They were then charged with conspiracy. It was a situation of real entrapment; it's highly unlikely their 'pipe dream' wish for an endless supply of cannabis would have been pursued without active police participation. If this were to occur nowadays, the prosecution of those involved would almost certainly not be able to proceed.

The case was unusual in another respect. The prosecution case against my client was, on my assessment, significantly weaker than that presented against any of the others in the group, as there was no evidence that he had taken any active step to further the plan and, other than his presence, little that indicated any contribution to their discussions. In that situation, I formed the view that our best chance was to emphasise his different position and separate him by being involved to the minimum extent possible in the conduct of the trial. It was a potentially dangerous strategy that depended upon nothing additional emerging in the evidence that might upset the balance or require active challenge or explanation.

Unsurprisingly, the client and his family began to lose confidence as the days passed and their counsel seemed to be, and in fact was, doing nothing that they could see, while those appearing for the co-accused were vigorously defending their clients. Despite my own increasing anxiety about the wisdom of this course, I ostentatiously declined over the ten days of the trial to cross-examine any witness, advance any objections to evidence, call any witnesses or join with the other counsel in presenting arguments, until final addresses.

The other accused were found guilty while, to my considerable relief, my client was acquitted. The jury, it seems, accepted our contention that there was no evidence that he had taken any active part and was, at most, minimally connected because he was present on some occasion when others were discussing what was, in any event, a ridiculous enterprise that had almost no chance of success.

The largest quantity of drugs involved in the various trials in which I was engaged was six tons of cannabis, which a Calabrian 'Ndrangheta-connected family had grown on a farm in northern Victoria. The prosecution contended that my clients, a married couple, had travelled from interstate to supervise the harvesting of the crop. They had made no admissions and there was little to incriminate them or rebut their claim that they were merely visiting relatives at the time of the police raid, so they were acquitted.

Following this successful outcome, I was offered further briefs to represent various individuals with whom they were linked in some way or other, but I did not want to be associated with this area and avoided accepting them.

*

Sometimes there are suggestions that a particular lawyer is so gifted that they never seem to lose cases. Usually, this claim means that the individual concerned does not undertake difficult cases or may perhaps have a short or defective memory that excludes their losses. One highly competent criminal advocate jokingly told me he felt embarrassed when he came into chambers because it seemed to be full of people who, unlike him, always won. Maybe such people exist, but I do not know of any, and it's certainly not a claim I can make. It was always a little confronting when I encountered unsuccessful clients in prison in my later Parole Board role. When I told one of them that I could not be involved in his case, he said, with an air of disappointment, that I had not been much help at his trial and he had hoped I would be more useful now.

While I often had grave doubts concerning a client's truthfulness or asserted state of mind and motivation, and in some cases developed a strong dislike of them, I presented their cases as well as I could. If the jury rejected their version, apart from some possible disappointment that I hadn't personally succeeded, I normally felt comfortable that I had done my best to ensure that a fair trial had been held, and their defence properly and forcefully put for the jury's consideration. There was only one occasion where I had serious doubts about the verdict, although even then the jury view was understandable and may have been right. The accused was undoubtedly guilty of the manslaughter of his victim, but he told so many lies to evade responsibility that his final explanation of what had taken place was rejected and he was convicted of murder. It is rare for miscarriages of justice to arise because of jury behaviour or errors made by them, and almost always attributable to judicial error.

Sometimes, I experienced a sense of unreality about the criminal trial process in which I was engaged. In a few cases involving professional criminals, it seemed highly likely that both my client *and* the police witnesses were lying. The trial was something of a charade, played out within a framework according to rules and for reasons known only to them. One of my clients was furious when he heard the police evidence of the amount of cash recovered in a raid on his house. I formed the impression that it was much less than he expected and that he believed they had taken some for themselves, but as he denied having any connection with it or the sawn-off shotgun in the same bag, he sat silently fuming.

Among the most worrying non-capital cases in which I appeared was one where the judge raised the possibility of imposing whipping as part of the penalty. At the end of the trial at which my client, a repeat offender, was convicted of a particularly violent kidnapping and armed robbery, the judge asked for submissions because he was contemplating making such an order. It had been almost twenty years since a prisoner had been whipped in Victoria, and I could hardly believe that this barbaric punishment was still being considered. The case was adjourned and, after further evidence and extensive argument, he did not persist.

Not long afterwards, I was in another case in the Supreme Court in which it was raised as a possibility by a different judge, but with less likelihood it would be ordered. The issue had arisen because the Chief Justice, Sir Edmund Herring who, as I indicated earlier, was a dreadful human being, suggested in a case before him that the punishment should be revived.

Although most of the criminal cases in which I was engaged involved serious behaviour or personal consequences, some possessed almost comic aspects. A movement in Victoria which was widely supported among the Croatian community was seeking separation from the Serbian-controlled Yugoslavia which had been established at the end of the Second World War.

As part of its monitoring of the activities of this group, the Australian Security Intelligence Organisation (ASIO) established a watching post in a house directly opposite the building occupied by a Croatian soccer club. Listening devices were planted, and additional expensive camera equipment was hired and placed in position to record comings and goings.

None of this was a secret to the Croatian community leaders, as ASIO would have known, and a comfortable equilibrium existed. However, it was broken when, during an afternoon function at the centre, some young men detected the camera, which had been positioned rather clumsily. Angered, a large group of them entered the building and took the equipment and recordings. The police were called, nearby streets were blocked off, and the covert surveillance operation descended into a noisy farce involving a large crowd of protesters and curious bystanders. The only charges laid related to the taking of the camera and recordings, which an embarrassed ASIO was concerned to recover. Newspaper reports of the incident emphasised my submission to the court that it was unfortunate that the movie character, James Bond, was apparently having a day off.

*

My work for some years after I started came mostly from suburban firms and included small civil disputes, contested and uncontested divorce proceedings, claims for maintenance by wives and single mothers, some workers compensation matters and criminal defence work. It wasn't generally high-level litigation, and I was certainly not an overnight success, but I was earning enough to keep going: the cases were important to those involved, and I learned much from them.

Quite a few disputes involved what were called 'protected tenancies'. These were rental arrangements under which, due to the length of the period of occupancy, the tenants had much greater rights under the law against termination.

In one of these cases, I represented an elderly female client who had lived in the same house for over forty years. She told me that not only did she want to stay in her home but also that her financial situation would not enable her to find somewhere else suitable. After negotiating with the property owner's lawyers, I secured a rather large payment for her, and she agreed to vacate. She thanked me profusely, saying she had been going to her local church every day and praying that God would help her because she did not want to go to court and tell lies. It transpired she was well off and was not at all troubled about leaving but wanted the best deal possible. I was amused by the revelation that God had apparently intervened on her behalf to avoid perjury. Before she left, she told me that she would pray for me. I thanked her, but wasn't sure God would be inclined to do her any more favours.

The smallest case I handled involved a teaspoon of condensed milk. One of the waterside workers had apparently taken a can from cargo being loaded onto a ship and left it beside the urn for their morning tea. When my client was seen helping himself to a spoonful, he was charged with receiving stolen property. The major consequence of conviction would have been the automatic loss of his registration with the body that regulated labour engagement in the industry, so it was important from his perspective. The magistrate, I think rather kindly, accepted my argument that there was no evidence that he knew that the particular can had been taken from the cargo, although in the circumstances it did seem likely.

Another client was charged with assault by kicking when he struck out at a man with his prosthetic leg. The magistrate quickly accepted that it was not legally possible to kick with an artificial limb. Considerably more difficulty was encountered, and a different outcome, when I submitted to a court that the definition of 'weapon' in the offence of assault with a weapon did not include the half barracuda that my fishmonger client used against a health inspector who queried whether it was fresh.

Some of the situations in which my clients placed or found themselves were extraordinary. One was a petty thief who, given the chance, would take anything that caught his eye. He was in a hotel one night with a group of other people when he noticed a bag underneath the bar. He waited until no one was looking and made off with it. Without checking inside, he placed the bag in his car and returned to his companions. When the hotel closed, the group dispersed, and he drove off. A short time later, as his behaviour patterns were well known by the local police, he was stopped by a patrol and the bag was opened. It contained the hotel's takings. The police took him back to the hotel, where they found members of the staff busily engaged in tying each other up for the purpose of staging a robbery. He had inadvertently stolen the money from the would-be thieves!

Another with similar propensities and whose determination far exceeded his abilities, decided to take the money held in a safe at his workplace. He went there at night and loaded the safe onto a trolley, which he was wheeling away when the police caught him. While on bail and undeterred by his arrest, about a fortnight later he returned to the building and tried to open the safe with an explosive. Having no idea of the amount to use, he blasted it through a wall and shredded the contents. When the police went to his home some hours later, they found him attempting to tape together pieces of banknotes.

Two others went to a department store for pantyhose with which they intended to conceal their faces during the robbery of a nearby bank. The shop assistant assumed they were purchasing a present and sold them two pair of an expensive and very sheer brand. The effect was to give them the appearance of a light tan but didn't impede recognition when the police examined the bank's video.

Robberies were almost always terrifying for those caught up as victims or witnesses, but I had one case where the armed robber of a betting agency was pushed to one side by a desperate punter determined to place his bet before the race started.

*

As I did not have a secretary, Dawn would type any documents I required. These included divorce petitions and civil pleadings. Our financial position remained uncertain because, although I did receive briefs in murder trials and some other substantial cases, I still did not have any reliable sources of work. But we were happy.

We secured a bank loan for a deposit to purchase a home and moved into a weatherboard house on a steeply sloping block directly across a valley from the airport at Essendon. John Coldrey and his wife Karin were living only a couple of streets away. John used to describe the area as 'the Paris end of Glenroy'. To see this connection with a mostly undeveloped thistle-covered hillside at the fringe of urban development required considerable imagination. But our house had floor-to-ceiling windows across the front that provided a wonderful view towards the city, and there were three bedrooms, one of which we prepared as a nursery. With the consent of the vendors, before taking possession we went there most evenings and painted the whole interior. Dawn also made curtains and covered a kitchen bench front. Neither of our families had ever owned their own home; we had always lived in rented accommodation, so it was additionally special.

On our first night after moving in, we were suddenly awakened by a terrible noise. When we subsequently learned that aircraft engines were sometimes tested at airport workshops in the early hours of the morning we were horrified, but soon developed the ability to sleep through it.

Our first pets were acquired: a cat that we named Simba and a beautiful Shetland sheepdog puppy called Manny. The seller had already entered Manny in a forthcoming dog show and persuaded us to take him along. When, to our surprise, he won, we decided to become involved in this activity. He was a beautiful dog and continued to win prizes, including best in his class at the Royal Melbourne Show. We stopped entering Manny when it became clear he had begun to hate it. Instead of prancing around the show ring, he would look completely miserable.

Dawn and I remained in that house until after our daughter Kerry was born; pushing a pram up and down the extremely steep driveway was dangerous, and it was unsafe to attempt to carry her.

With all its limitations, I have wonderful memories of our time there and I came to understand what my father meant to convey when he spoke of 'closing the door'.

Our next home, which was on the other side of the city, was much better in every respect other than the view. I was delighted and regarded it as a real sign of progress when, not long after we moved in, we had central heating installed.

WORKERS COMPENSATION

I had received occasional briefs in workers compensation cases from my earliest days, but they did not constitute a significant part of my work until I was 'discovered' by solicitors acting for insurance companies after a fortuitous encounter. It was late one afternoon towards the end of 1969, and I was returning to my room from a suburban court. A law clerk who had previously worked for Clyde Holding with Dawn and me was at the entrance of the building just as I happened to pass by. He said the counsel who would normally be engaged by his firm to represent their insurance company clients in cases at the Workers Compensation Board had suffered a heart attack, and asked whether I would be available to take over some cases that were listed for hearing on the following morning. I didn't have a brief for that day and was happy to accept.

On my arrival at the Board, other solicitors who had also engaged that barrister were looking for someone. A few days later, after I had handled the cases for them, they asked whether I would undertake part of their work on an ongoing basis. I happily accepted and rushed home that afternoon to tell Dawn that, within just one week I had unexpectedly acquired the opportunity to develop a substantial practice.

Finally, there was the prospect of a secure income source. A great deal would have to be done to consolidate the position, including gaining a deeper understanding of the medical areas and industrial processes upon which claims were based. But this was not regarded as posing a problem, and I was familiar with the jurisdiction generally. However, after years of uncertainty, I was apprehensive about becoming too dependent on particular solicitors or on a single type of case, and continued to accept briefs in other areas when available. But that work declined as I became more and more involved until, except for occasional Public Solicitor murder trials, I was essentially fully engaged. There is always a degree of luck involved in any change of fortune, and that was the case here. Had I arrived a few minutes earlier or later, our life situation could have been very different.

The process of securing the seriously inadequate amounts available as compensation for injured workers or their dependants was problematic for a number of reasons. Most of the contested claims were concerned with medical and factual causation and, often, the outcome would depend on the Board's view of the evidence given by well paid 'hired gun' medical experts from each side. They would line up against each other in a kind of ritual dance, and as soon as the names of the doctors who had been engaged were known, it was possible to predict with a high level of confidence the cases that would be presented by the opposing parties.

Much of the heavy physical work in the community in the period following the Second World War was being done by migrants from Europe, particularly Italy, and many of those who were injured came from that country. They often had little understanding of our legal system, and in an endeavour to communicate with some very anxious people and demonstrate my commitment to their cases, I undertook Italian language lessons for two years. Dawn joined me in this and we would go to classes and practise together. I think the clients appreciated my clumsy attempts to talk directly with them.

Most of the claims were based on genuine injury or disease, but there were a few that were not. One involved a criminal who claimed to have injured his back at work. Given his deep aversion to lawful physical activity, there was considerable doubt about whether he had suffered any injury at all, and certainly about the circumstances on which his claim was based. This induced a not particularly smart insurance investigator to attempt to set a trap for him. He placed a twenty dollar note on the ground in front of the claimant's house but concerned it might blow away in the wind, he put a small stone on it to keep it in place. The claimant emerged and saw both the note and the stone. He smiled and stood there until, after asking a passing child to assist him to pick it up, he waved the note in the air and happily went on his way.

Ironically, he later suffered a genuine back injury in a motor accident, but could make only a limited claim because he was already supposedly disabled to almost the same extent. Always eager to seize an opportunity, he offered, when I went to see him in hospital, to approach other patients who might require a lawyer—for a small commission, of course. He was a little disappointed at my lack of interest in his proposition. In another case, an investigator filmed a person, who unsurprisingly resembled the claimant because he was his brother, catching heavy pumpkins being thrown to him on a truck but missed the claimant, who was throwing them.

Perhaps the most unusual claim was made by the dependants of a man who died while sitting in his lounge room at his home during a New Year's Eve party. He was due to commence a shift at midnight and, in order to secure compensation for his family, helpful, and probably inebriated, guests dressed him in his work clothes, prepared sandwiches for his meal break and took his body from the house and propped it against a fence to be discovered by some passerby. The plan fell apart when one of those involved became alarmed and disclosed what had happened.

Another extraordinary workers compensation case involved a back injury. The claimant asserted he was confined to his bed, and his evidence was given at his home. He said he had begun to experience back pain at work that increased in intensity until he collapsed shortly after leaving a railway station on his way home at around lunchtime on a Saturday. He then crawled for what would have been at least half a kilometre along a busy footpath, ignored by passersby, until he reached a local doctor's surgery. While still on his knees, he knocked on the door, but was turned away. He then moved painfully to a fire station further down the street and asked to use their telephone and, again, was refused assistance. He then crawled several blocks to his home. On its face, this was a remarkable story and was viewed by the insurer for which I was briefed as, at least, a highly exaggerated description of what had occurred, if not entirely untrue.

Before I went home after the hearing, I called in to see my mother, who was living in the area, and told her about this extraordinary evidence. She expressed no surprise and said it certainly could have happened. The particular doctor's surgery was always closed on Saturdays for religious reasons and even very ill people were often turned away. Troubled by the possibility I had been trying to cast doubt on what may well have been a truthful version, after I left her, I drove to the fire station. A couple of the men there remembered this strange occurrence. They said a man they dismissed as drunk had crawled in one day and asked to use their phone, and they had told him to go away. Obviously, it would have been unethical to withhold this knowledge. I informed his lawyer of what I had learned, and the claim was settled. As a judge, I always regarded this case as a powerful reminder of the importance of not drawing conclusions too quickly.

PRESSURE

For the next couple of years, things appeared to be going well for Dawn and me. There was a continuing flow of well-paid work and some murder trials so, for the first time, we were financially comfortable. Our other daughter, Lisa, was born, and we had an overseas holiday.

But external and internal pressures were beginning to accumulate. Dawn's father had developed throat cancer, and as he became increasingly incapacitated, she became concerned about him and her mother. At the same time, my own father's health deteriorated. The two men died within twelve months of each other, both aged 61.

I became dissatisfied with the workers compensation jurisdiction. My practice consisted of representing widows of deceased workers, individuals who had suffered serious injury or contracted industrial diseases as my father had or, to a lesser extent, acting for insurance companies to contest their claims. It was common for me to handle two and sometimes three cases in a day. Few were the subject of a full hearing, with most being negotiated within a narrow range of payments.

The injuries sustained were frequently of a mental health character and, because they could not be objectively demonstrated, they tended to be viewed with suspicion. Yet they were often seriously disabling and sometimes compounded the effect of physical injury. Among the worst of the cases I handled were those in which the worker had committed suicide. Liability was normally denied by the insurers, who would argue that employment could not be shown to have played a significant part in the worker's decision and that there may have been other factors involving their health, personal situations and relationships. I detested these cases and the necessary exploration of issues that could be grossly offensive and hurtful to their families who frequently were struggling with life-shattering events.

By contrast, there were some curious arbitrary consequences arising from the entitlement system for compensation. An employee who fell off his bike and was injured on his way home from work would be covered if it happened outside his front gate but not if he had landed inside the boundary. In one of my cases, a worker who was trying to catch pigeons fell through the roof, was found to be at his place of employment when he sustained his injuries on the floor below.

I would receive much more income from these briefs than I would for a Public Solicitor funded murder trial and for a while I was delighted by our improved financial situation. However, I soon became dissatisfied by my involvement in an absurd system that benefited principally those involved in its operation. My desire to be a 'real' advocate gradually increased until I felt I had to move on. In frustration, I returned from the Board one day in early 1973 and handed back all the briefs I then held. The situation was no less difficult for Dawn. In addition to sharing my problems, she had two young children and a growing desire to further her education and pursue her own career when they reached school age. She was also worried about her mother, who was obviously having trouble coping following the death of Dawn's father.

BACK TO CRIME

Suddenly, after eight years of struggle and uncertainty, I had developed a good practice in a lucrative area that I was now abandoning. The major difference in our situation was that I was, by that stage, seen as an experienced barrister and could anticipate securing criminal trial work. The transition was successful and within twelve months I was engaged principally in homicide cases, briefed by specialist criminal law firms and the Public Solicitor.

Until the end of 1974, the pronouncement of the sentence of death by the judge was mandatory on the conviction for murder of adult offenders. In consequence, judges were extremely reluctant to accept a plea of guilty. When a man in Victoria wanted to do this in the 1950s, the judge reserved his decision before concluding that it was even permissible.

It was considered essential that there should never be any room for doubt concerning the justice and legal correctness of the conviction. Therefore, the evidence had to be produced and assessed in a public hearing so that any determination of guilt or subsequent decisions by the State Executive Council, which had the power to direct execution or substitute imprisonment, could be seen to be properly based. The policy was based on the possibility that the accused, for their own reasons, might have falsely or incorrectly accepted responsibility for any of a wide range of unknown motivations.

I appeared for the defence in several cases where the evidence against my clients was overwhelming. My main objective in that situation was to ensure that anything that could be advanced on their behalf was emphasised. This was by no means treated as a formal process and all issues were fully contested. Particular attention was given to any mitigating features in an attempt to minimise the possibility of execution or to persuade the jury that, by exercising their constitutional prerogative of mercy, justice would be served by a verdict of manslaughter. Of course, in the majority of cases, a manslaughter verdict was arguable. At the time of the abolition of the death penalty, I had three clients whose death sentences had not yet been commuted to a term of imprisonment, although it was clear by then that they would be.

Young people under the age of eighteen years were not subject to the same regime and would be detained subject to the 'Governor's pleasure'. In practice, they were held in adult prison and released by Cabinet decision after serving a number of years. Later, as Chair of the Adult Parole Board, I attended one of the meetings at which this was done and participated in the discussions.

There were certainly far more lucrative and less demanding ways of making a living at the bar, but I never seriously pursued any of them. I became almost addicted to the pressure involved in cases that carried such enormous consequences, and saw this work as 'the only game in town'. Representation of the accused in a continuing series of difficult trials over the next ten years absorbed almost all my time and much of my emotional energy.

The prosecution in a criminal trial commences with the advantage that the members of the jury will reasonably anticipate there is a strong likelihood that accused are guilty, otherwise they would not be on trial and that the prosecutor is seeking justice for the community and those directly affected. The defence endeavours to diminish this impression by personalising the situation of the individual before them, presenting a different perspective and emphasising deficiencies in the evidence and argument being advanced against them, and arguing that justice requires acquittal.

Most members of the community, I suspect, gain their images of violence from television, movies and books, but often what occurs is much more banal. Of course, highly intelligent, socially sophisticated criminals exist and prey on our community; however, the great majority of those who come before the courts are far from that. We are reluctant to acknowledge they are not only part of our society but, frequently and at least partly, the product of our own failures. Crime provides a distorted mirror image of ourselves and our asserted values: to some extent revealing aspects that we do not want to recognise and some for which we are unprepared to accept responsibility. Those who engage in it do not come from some other planet but from within us.

Among the features of most situations in which individuals in our community kill others is the almost infantile primitivism and power of the emotions that motivate much human behaviour and deprive the actor of any appreciation of the dreadful character and consequences, even to themselves, of the choice being made. A love-struck eighteen-year-old who shot his rival told me, 'You will never understand, she is the only woman I could ever love.' Saddened by the adolescent naivety of this earnest explanation of an act that resulted in such dreadful consequences, there was nothing I could usefully say in response.

I observed this emotional power time after time in cases of violence where males were unable to accept their partner's right to personal integrity and decision-making, as to do so would have threatened their fragile sense of identity and self-worth. Their view of the controlling role and entitlements of men in personal relationships has been deeply embedded and, until recently, largely unchallenged in our society and law over many centuries. Sadly, although its power is diminishing, it persists, resulting in a great many deaths as well as many other destructive manifestations.

In the relatively small number of cases in which I was involved where women subject to domestic violence reacted by killing their partners, it seemed to me they had engaged in acts of revolution against oppression and that the forces driving them were quite different. One of my clients had tolerated extreme violence, humiliation and fear for many years in order to have a home for her children. This ended one night when her husband subjected them to the type of conduct she had endured. The rationale that enabled her to survive and tolerate years of abuse no longer applied and she killed him with one of the several knives that he had placed within easy reach around the house to intimidate her.

In another, a mother who had previously sought and failed to secure assistance, was concerned to protect her daughters from further sexual and physical abuse by their father. A crisis point was reached when one of the young girls had a knife placed at her throat and agreed to his demand for total obedience. Having no money and nowhere to go, she decided that her only option was to kill the oppressor while he slept.

In each of these situations, the women acted in the defence of their children. There were others in which they feared for themselves and saw their conduct as pre-emptive of anticipated attack and continued domination against which they considered they had no other effective defence. Our law now makes better allowance for such situations and increasing attention is being given to the problem of domestic violence, but, even at that time, jurors understood and acquitted them.

I appeared as the junior counsel in only two murder trials. In the first, our client was an extremely disturbed young man who had killed an elderly Salvation Army couple. He had met them a little over an hour or so earlier, when they saw him hitch-hiking as they were driving by and offered him a lift to the city. On the way, they passed near his home, and he asked them to stop and wait for a couple of minutes. He returned with a shotgun and forced them to drive to a remote area, where he killed them and drove their car back and forth over their bodies. It was an extraordinarily violent crime, committed seemingly without reason.

At the time, we were aware the victims were connected with the Bayswater Boys' Home operated by the Salvation Army where our client had been detained as a young boy. His hatred of two people he had never previously met and who engaged in charitable work for the purpose of assisting young people seemed inexplicable and was regarded as the product of his disturbed mental state. Our endeavours to ascertain his motivation were met with extreme resistance and he never provided a reason other than a general dislike of the home. The exposure of the terrible abuses that occurred there did not emerge until many years later.

After the trial, he was placed in J Ward for the insane at Ararat, where I saw him from time to time. I wonder whether—although he never hinted of anything of that kind—he was a victim of child abuse and his murder of this couple one of its consequences. As a judge, I presided over the trial of four men charged with the bombing of police headquarters in Russell Street, Melbourne. Two of them, I later learned, were the victims of abuse as children in the same institution. It is likely to be a long time before the spreading ripples of personal tragedy from this widespread abuse are stilled.

In the second of these murder trials in which I appeared as junior counsel, our client was tried for the execution murder of the secretary of one of the waterfront unions. The killing occurred in the course of one of the three major underworld conflicts with which I had some connection while in practice.

The accused was a young man with a background of severe deprivation and a relatively minor criminal history. He had met the instigator, a man named William Longley, while in prison and had become something of a protégé to him. Longley was engaged in a struggle for control of the union and associated criminal activities, with the secretary being seen as an obstacle. No difficulty was encountered in carrying out the killing which was carefully orchestrated. The victim was induced to meet some other people in a hotel and sit at a particular table where he would be exposed. Once he was identified, our client who was armed with a rifle entered and shot him.

Although the police denied ever receiving any such information, it seems likely that the person given the role of identifying the victim, fearing for his own position, had informed them of the plot well beforehand and those involved were soon arrested. He also assisted them in the recovery of the rifle that had been thrown into the Yarra. When this was produced in the course of the police interview of our client, he made a number of important admissions that resulted in his conviction. I was not involved in the subsequent trial when our client was later charged and acquitted of the murder, while in prison, of this co-offender.

Aged three years

With Brian at Melbourne Zoo

With Brian at Station 7LA, Launceston

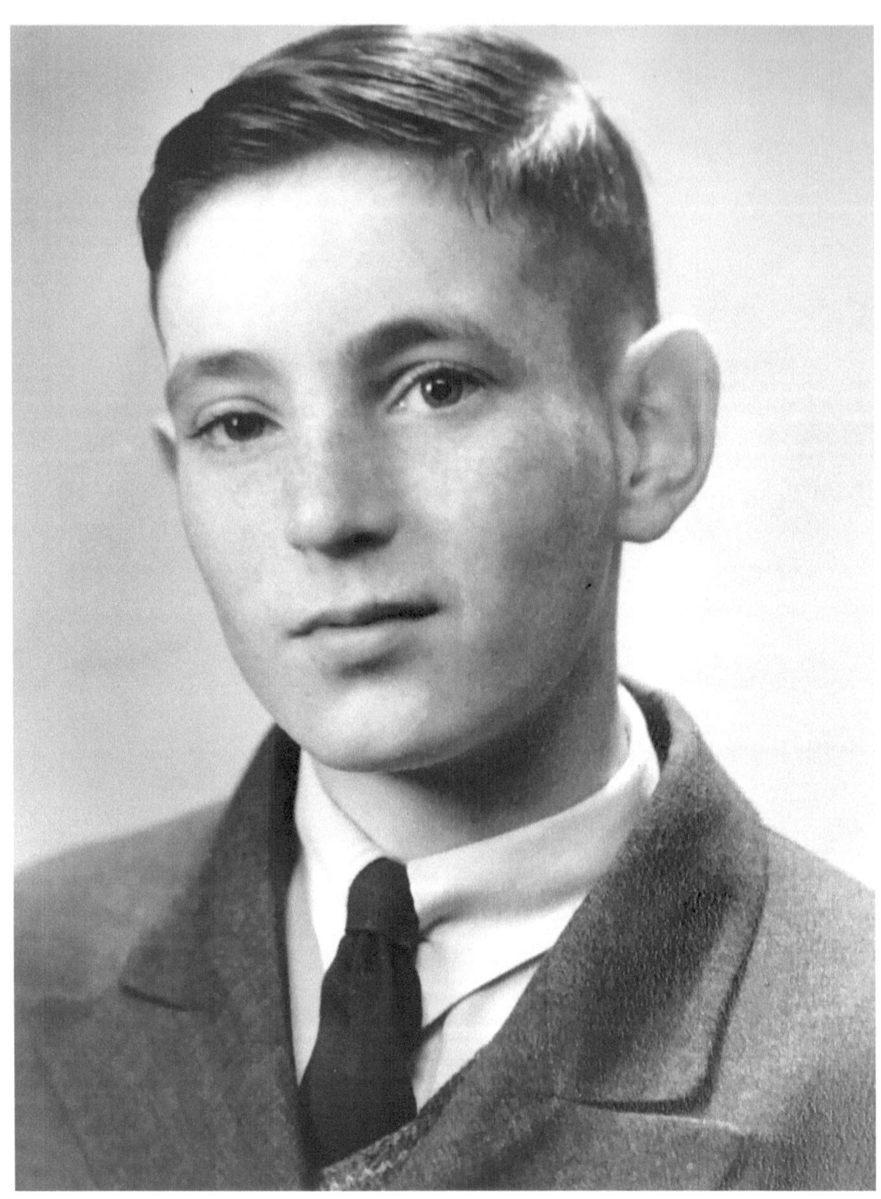

Aged eleven at St Patrick's College, Launceston

My mother (left), aged sixteen, and her sister on tour with magic show

Judith on her wedding day with our mother

My father with a broken arm in union demonstration

My mother as a young woman

Dawn, aged eight years

Just married

With Dawn, 1965

Central Australian Legal Aid, 1974

Dawn at Coober Pedy on way to Alice Springs, 1977

Going to court at Yuendumu
in 1976

With Kerry and Lisa
on Bathurst Island

Dressed for court

With my family on installation as Chancellor of VU

Retirement

ALICE SPRINGS

Another development around this time had profound consequences for my career and the lives of Dawn and myself. A good friend, Geoff Eames, who had taken up the position of senior lawyer at the recently established Central Australian Aboriginal Legal Aid Service—and years later joined me on the Supreme Court—asked me to appear for the accused in Alice Springs in the middle of 1974 in the first murder trial handled by the Service. I accepted with no inkling of the changes this decision would precipitate.

Within minutes of my arrival there, some of the problems with which the Aboriginal community was grappling became obvious. On the way into town from the airport, I saw people living in terrible conditions in shelters constructed of rusty galvanised iron and other cast-off materials in the dry bed of the Todd River. Altogether, it presented a saddening scene and was indicative of their depressed state.

I had just arrived at the Legal Aid office when a group from a nearby settlement appeared: they were seeking help to recover money that they were confident had been misappropriated by the Government-appointed manager. They had no records to support their belief and only a vague idea of how much may have been involved. In the circumstances, Geoff and I decided a direct approach was probably our best first step, and we went to the manager's home. When he answered the door, we simply stated we were from Legal Aid and demanded he hand over the community's money. To our surprise, he asked us to wait, went inside and returned with a box containing cash and a few scrappy records. I had grave doubts we had recovered more than a small part of what had been taken, but the community was satisfied with the outcome, and so we had to let the matter drop.

The Legal Aid Service had booked me into a motel, but I felt uncomfortable about this use of their limited funds, so I moved out and slept on the lounge room floor at Geoff's home. With Geoff, his wife and their two children, two other Legal Aid lawyers, an Aboriginal family of four and me, the house was packed.

Our client was charged with the murder of a respected local Aboriginal man during a brawl involving some town residents and a group from one of the outlying settlements. As well as our intention to ensure that his defence was properly put before the jury and that he was afforded his best chance of a successful outcome, we were conscious of the importance of establishing the Service as a professionally competent body.

The prosecution contention was that, after a fight had broken out in the bar, the settlement group had been forced outside and the doorway blocked. The accused, armed with a knife, had returned through another door and stabbed the victim in retaliation. We argued that the evidence, much of which was given by men who had been drinking heavily and were partisan in any event, was unreliable. The defence claim—that our client had acted in self-defence—failed, and he was convicted. However, I believe it became clear from that time that all involved in providing legal aid for the Aboriginal people in Central Australia were determined to provide the best service possible.

There was some suspicion in the Alice Springs community and, I think, among the judiciary at first about the intentions and motivation of the new lawyers. Many in the local white population perceived us as either politically motivated or troublemaking do-gooders from 'the south' with no understanding of the issues and life in the Territory. Much of this suspicion dissipated, certainly among the judges, once it became clear that our objective was to ensure that the rights provided under our legal system were actually, and not merely theoretically, available to the disadvantaged Aboriginal people of Central Australia. Nevertheless, it persisted in some sections of the community, and there were a few nasty incidents.

Ted Hill had once advised me to be careful about too readily espousing high-sounding principles because the time could arrive when I might be called upon to act on them. In Alice Springs, I encountered a small group of people who were endeavouring to ensure justice and advance the interests of some of the most disadvantaged people in our society. I was building my practice as a criminal advocate in Victoria and reluctant at a time when the relationship between Dawn and myself was under stress to spend time away, but felt obligated to assist.

From the moment of my first conference with an Aboriginal client, which was conducted under a tree outside the Legal Aid office, it was clear there was an enormous amount to learn. Almost none of my clients had even the most basic understanding of such matters as the elements of the crimes with which they were charged and their rights under the law. To communicate with them, even with the help of interpreters, required patience and considerable care. Even then, there was often doubt about the extent of their comprehension.

While usually going to the Northern Territory to represent the accused in jury trials, when there I would assist in the Magistrates' or Children's Courts, which were always busy. The lawyers would arrive at a court in the morning and frequently find twenty or thirty people waiting, many having been arrested overnight. Frequently, they had been badly affected by alcohol at the time of the alleged offence or when arrested and, in any event, had no understanding of the processes or even recollection of whether they may have done the things attributed to them. Obtaining useful instructions was often well-nigh impossible.

The prosecution cases were seldom well prepared. As the police themselves may not have been confident they had sufficient evidence and were unused to their word being tested by experienced criminal lawyers, they frequently withdrew the charges as soon as a plea of not guilty was announced. Occasionally, they made surprising admissions. Once, in cross-examination in the local court at Yuendumu (a settlement about three hundred kilometres to the west of Alice Springs), I put to the arresting officer that he had punched my client before interviewing him. With an air of surprise at the implication that I may have regarded this as somehow wrong, he responded that he certainly had.

I should point out that the maintenance of order and reasonable community relations by a lone and probably poorly trained police member living with his family in a small community a long way from available assistance should it be quickly required, such as Yuendumu, would have posed many challenges. Nevertheless, police attitudes across the Northern Territory towards Aboriginal people were generally bad. There was unconcealed racism, which, at its best, was reflected in a moderating paternalism but sometimes involved serious abuse and violence. One man that I subsequently represented in civil proceedings had been tied to a fence post and savagely beaten with a length of bamboo that left scars across his back, while another in an unconnected incident had been chained to a log outside a settlement police station and left sitting in the hot sun for hours.

The most serious of the cases involving claims of police violence towards Aboriginal men in which I was involved arose from an occurrence at Ti Tree, a small community located on the Stuart

Highway north of Alice Springs.

Following a confrontation between police and a group of men returning to a cattle station in the area about a week earlier, two police members, in an attempt to demonstrate their authority, stopped a car that they thought may have contained some of them. A fight developed during which one of the Aboriginal men, none of whom was armed, was shot dead and another seriously wounded. The men claimed they had been seized and assaulted by the two officers involved, and that, when they fought back, one of the police fired at them.

The surviving men were arrested and charged with attempted murder. My friend, John Coldrey, an English lawyer named Henry Spooner who was working at the Legal Aid Service at the time, and I represented them at their trial which was held in Darwin to secure an independent jury. Our clients were acquitted on the principal charge but convicted on minor charges of fighting. Subsequently, the police were committed and tried for murder in Alice Springs and also acquitted. I have always been troubled by the lack of interest outside the local community in the trial of two police for the murder of an Aboriginal man in these circumstances, and as late as the 1970s.

Recognition and enforcement of the rights of Aboriginal people under the law remained a serious problem. Relatively few had any real capacity to exercise them, if they knew what they were, which was unlikely. Even when an interviewing police member carefully explained they had the right to refuse to answer questions or incriminate themselves, they sometimes believed that they had no real choice. This perception was clearly expressed by a client who regarded the careful recitation of his rights by the interviewer as a meaningless ritual, believing that, if he refused to answer police questions, he would receive a 'hiding'. His understanding was not irrational and rested on a long history of the relationships between the authorities and the Indigenous population in a part of the country where, within living memory, Aboriginal people had been hunted down and killed.

In 1928, following the death of a white man who had been engaged in hunting wild dogs and without any serious investigation of the circumstances, an officially sanctioned revenge party indiscriminately rounded up a large number of the local Walpiri, Anmatyerre and Kaytete people. According to public records, in what became known as the Coniston massacre, seventeen were killed, but it seems clear and was believed by the Aboriginal community that the number was almost certainly much higher and may have exceeded one hundred. Although there was a formal Inquiry, no one was ever held to account for what took place.

Two Aboriginal men were subsequently charged with the murder of the dog hunter but were acquitted on the direction of the trial judge when it became clear that the evidence against them was fabricated. Constable Murray, a prosecution witness, when asked by the judge whether it was 'really necessary to shoot to kill in every case' responded, 'what is the use of a wounded blackfellow hundreds of miles from civilisation'. It was not until 1967 that our Indigenous population were even counted in the census. One of the survivors of Coniston was an elder involved in the operation of the Legal Service when I was there.

Considered against the background of that event which, of course, was part of a long history of violence against Aboriginal people across the Northern Territory, and their individual experiences of family and personal interactions with authority at all levels, it is hardly surprising that few were prepared to insist on their rights.

A very different manhunt but nevertheless with a potential for a tragic outcome took place at the time of one of my regular trips to Darwin. A group of Aboriginal men had escaped from Berimah prison and were hiding in the Port Keats area, a remote region approximately four hundred kilometres to the south-west where there was a Catholic mission. A heavily armed police party was dispatched to apprehend them. The escapees did not appear to be dangerous but there was a risk of confrontation. The senior lawyer at the Legal Service, Colin McDonald, who had been one of my bar readers, was concerned to avoid this if possible and negotiate their safe return to custody so the two of us went to the mission. While the police were receiving the dubious assistance of the local people who, despite their familiarity with the area and the escapees, never seemed able to find them, we made contact through the community elders and arranged for them to return to custody without incident. When I pointed out the holes in the walls of the old mission building in which we were staying, I was jokingly told that they were too small for the local mosquitoes. They were not.

There was such broad acceptance within the Aboriginal people of the power of the police and authority generally that, even after the establishment of the legal service, their word was rarely challenged or the right against self-incrimination asserted. The police could reasonably anticipate that they would plead guilty and little care in the preparation of cases was taken until it became clear that cases would be seriously contested.

The extent of the disregard of not just the rights but the humanity of Aboriginal people that could occur even in the late 1970s became clear when an American couple contacted the Legal Service. They were returning to the US. and wanted to adopt and take an Aboriginal child in their care with them. This required the signature of the child's mother on the necessary documentation, and they did not know her whereabouts. Ross Howie, the senior lawyer, immediately realised that something was drastically amiss and commenced inquiries. It was discovered that the child had been placed in care when his mother was in hospital. She was given no information and returned to her remote community believing he had been taken by the authorities as so many others had been. Once the situation became clear, the Service was able to secure his return to his family.

Consistent with a pervasive sense of powerlessness within the Aboriginal community when confronted with white authority and the operation of a system which was a mystery to them, I arrived at court one day to discover my client's brother in the dock. Although he had no idea why he had been arrested, he did not challenge the police and simply accepted that everything would eventually be made clear.

In one trial in which I was engaged, seven Aboriginal men were accused of participation in the rape of a woman in Alice Springs. Records of interview containing admissions of guilt by each of them were produced that, incredibly, were identically worded, save for necessary variations in the identity of the person allegedly confessing and the transposition of alleged actors' names. Even more extraordinary, in these interviews, all of the accused implicated a person who, it became clear beyond dispute, was never present at any relevant time or involved in anything that had occurred. The police would indicate the place where the confession was to be signed or an adopting mark made by tapping it with the barrel of a revolver.

This case, and another I was involved in, where several Aboriginal men were charged with murder, and the argument for the defence was presented by Ian Barker, QC, resulted in the establishment by the Supreme Court of the Northern Territory of a new system of support for Aboriginal persons when being interviewed by police. It was designed to ensure they were adequately informed of their rights and, as a practical proposition, able to exercise them. Some years later as a member of the Court of Criminal Appeal in Victoria, I participated in the decision that the same approach was required when interviewing persons with intellectual disability. They were similarly vulnerable to injustice in that situation.

In some ways, the issues we had to grapple with during the early operation of the Service were more straightforward than those encountered later. The mere fact that there was now a body committed to ensuring the adequate representation of Indigenous people in our legal system represented a vast improvement. As time has passed, the expression and manifestations of discrimination have evolved and they are now not so overtly primitive and therefore more difficult to address.

Representation in cases of multiple accused could present problems. There was neither sufficient money nor were there enough experienced lawyers readily available to provide separate counsel in every case but, fortunately, there were only a few where conflicts of interest could be seen and separate representation would be arranged. In the others, it was still difficult to ensure that the individual circumstances of the clients received proper attention, particularly where there were different levels of involvement alleged against them. I was always troubled by the obvious tension involved in arguing forcibly for each without diminishing the overall effect or compromising the position of their co-accused. It was clearly unsatisfactory, but there was often no practical alternative.

Even with the help of an interpreter, securing instructions from clients about whether to plead guilty—perhaps to a less serious charge—could be difficult in cases where the likely outcome of a contested trial was uncertain and the potential consequences were dramatically different. This was almost always due to their difficulty in coping with what was to them a foreign system based on legal principles expressed in terms that often confuse those who are familiar with them and conducted in a language they had difficulty following. Sometimes the choices they had to make arose in the context of a trial for murder with three variably probable outcomes: conviction for murder, manslaughter or total acquittal. The prospects and potential consequences of each had to be assessed against those involved in a plea of guilty to manslaughter, which the prosecutor indicated would be accepted.

It was a situation I encountered in many cases and a wide range of offences and consequences involving Aboriginal and non-Aboriginal clients in Victoria. Usually, they would have at least some basic understanding of the legal situation and their prospects of success in a trial upon which they could make an assessment, and have discussed their options with family members or friends. Even then, while every effort was made to ensure that they understood the nature and possible consequences of the adoption of the choices available to them, it was impossible to avoid the influence that our advice or assessment might have.

When one of my Victorian clients asked for my view of the prospects of a successful defence, I informed him that they were poor. He thanked me profusely and immediately absconded. He was caught two years later. Another, after leaving my room in Owen Dixon Chambers on a Friday morning where we had been discussing aspects of the case against him, was walking across the road to the Supreme Court that was located directly opposite when he panicked and hailed a passing taxi. He had been on bail throughout and the trial was going well. It seemed likely that he would be acquitted, so the judge adjourned the hearing to give me the opportunity to get him back. About two hours later, the client rang, apologising and obviously drunk. He assured me that he would be there when it resumed. Over the weekend, I was running in a marathon when I saw him at the edge of the road cheering me on. As promised, he came to my room on the next morning. This time, I walked across with him. Nothing was said to the jury and the trial continued, resulting in his expected release.

The problem of securing instructions became particularly

acute in these Central Australian cases because the clients—often having no knowledge whatever of the legal and evidentiary framework within which their choice had to be made and insufficient confidence to ask questions or articulate their concerns—would be relying much more heavily on their legal advisers. This was an unwanted but sometimes unavoidable responsibility, and the utmost care was required. The client would bear the consequences and it was important to try to communicate the potential risks and outcomes of the adoption of the available courses. Frequently, I was unsure when using interpreters who also had limited understanding of the system whether they understood and were correctly communicating what was being said.

Sometimes the way our legal system operated left the Aboriginal clients totally confused. One that I represented in a manslaughter trial in Alice Springs indicated that he thought the process was mad. He had been in custody from the time of his arrest and the judge had already indicated to the prosecutor and myself that he would not impose any further imprisonment on conviction. The jury had been deliberating for a long time and a disagreement seemed likely. If that occurred, the prosecutor informed me, the charge would be dropped.

To reduce the obvious anxiety of my client and his wife, it was explained, through an interpreter, that there were three possible outcomes, and all would result in his immediate release. He might be convicted, and the judge would almost certainly not impose any further imprisonment; he might be found not guilty, and would, of course, be immediately freed; finally, the prosecutor had informed me that if jury disagreed, the case would be dropped.

Once my client understood the position, he made it clear that he regarded his detention for many months and the conduct of the trial as an absurd ritual and queried why it was necessary to wait for the verdict. As it was a typical hot day, the accused and all others involved in the case, except the judge and jury, sat under some trees outside the court house and shared a couple of cartons of beer while we waited for the verdict. The jury did not arrive at a decision and the prosecution was dropped.

In a less serious situation, where two brothers were charged in relation to an offence that they committed together, they had extreme difficulty in accepting that the difference in the admissible evidence meant that one would go free while the other had no defence. The notions of the burden and standard of proof in a criminal proceeding, with which we are familiar from an early age in western society, were foreign to them in more than one sense.

Gaining access to individuals in custody was hard at first but improved substantially following a remarkable personal intervention by the Commonwealth Attorney-General, Lionel Murphy. The policing role in the Northern Territory was performed by the Australian Federal Police at that time and he was the responsible Minister. Rather than becoming enmeshed in the bureaucracy which at best would have delayed a response beyond the point that it would been of value to the young man, or subsequently challenging the admission of any statement he may have made, a telephone call had been made to his office by Geoff Eames. To our surprise, within minutes the Attorney-General personally rang the Alice Springs Police Station and made it clear he expected obstruction to the exercise of the rights of persons in custody to stop.

At the same time that I started to become involved in this work, my life otherwise was unravelling. Both Dawn and I were continuing to be affected by the ongoing personal and family pressures. The situation came to a head when a client I defended in the Supreme Court was convicted of murder and sentenced to death. I was shocked by this outcome as I was confident that we could secure a verdict of manslaughter, and concerned that I had badly misjudged the position or the significance of some of the evidence.

Although there was almost no chance that he would be executed—it was clear the death penalty was soon to be abolished—I was extremely troubled. I had of course been unsuccessful in other murder cases, but this trial had much greater impact, largely due to the extent to which the client was heavily dependent upon me in relation to all aspects of his representation. He was a derelict who had killed another in a fight over a bottle of cheap fortified wine worth a few dollars. I had advised him that his prospects of success were good so he rejected the opportunity to plead guilty to manslaughter and to proceed to trial on that basis. I kept asking myself—was he paying the price for my overconfidence?

The sense of responsibility involved in such cases when you begin to doubt your own judgement can result in real difficulty with strategic and tactical decision-making and increase dramatically the already high level of stress involved. The judge's words as he pronounced the death sentence kept echoing in my mind for many years afterwards. I subsequently encountered this client in the prison system on Parole Board visits. He accepted the verdict as correct and, while I could recall every detail of his trial, having played it over in my mind many times, he did not remember me.

Devastated by the outcome in this trial, I decided to leave the bar and commenced at the recently established Victorian Aboriginal Legal Aid Service in Fitzroy as a solicitor at the end of 1974.

Dawn was also struggling. She was unhappy that her education had been interrupted by polio and that she had not completed secondary level schooling. She was appreciative of the sacrifices that her parents had made for her and their decision to send her to a private secretarial college, but felt that she could achieve more, and wanted to develop a career path for herself once the children were at school. So, she commenced to undertake the final two years by correspondence. It was certainly not easy and involved a great deal of study and written work at night when the children were sleeping. At the same time, she was endeavouring to support her mother, who was coping badly on her own after Dawn's father died and becoming heavily dependent upon her.

Things quickly came to a head between us as we grappled with our individual issues and the pressures they placed on our relationship. We were unhappy, and I moved out. Looking back, it is apparent that, although painful, this period enabled us to come together later in a more powerful union that I doubt would have been achievable otherwise.

I remained at the Victorian Aboriginal Legal Aid Service for only a few months and returned to Alice Springs, where I started to work with Geoff Eames. However, I was extremely unsettled, and hated being away from Dawn and the children. I quickly realised that the solution to our difficulties was not going to be found in physical distance. I returned to Melbourne and the bar, and soon afterwards moved into a flat in Armadale, which I shared with my sister, Judith, for the next four years. She was employed by one of the television stations in program production and worked in that industry for several years before qualifying and practising as a clinical psychologist.

Dawn went well in her exams and commenced at Monash University as a part-time student. She later graduated with two degrees, one in arts and the other an honours degree in social work. It took enormous application in difficult circumstances for her to achieve what she did.

I did not expect to go again to the Northern Territory after returning to the bar, and may not have done so if I had not been called back concerning an incident that had occurred at the Finke township, approximately four hundred and fifty kilometres to the south of Alice Springs.

It had occurred a few days before I returned to Melbourne and developed after a group of Aboriginal men—who were sitting quietly in the shade of a water tower built for the 'Ghan', a passenger and freight train that operates between Adelaide and Central Australia—were ordered away by railway crew using abusive racist language. One of them, who had previously served time in prison for violence and was known by the colourful nickname of Cyanide, objected to the way he and the other men were being treated and refused to move, employing his equally extensive vocabulary of colloquial terms of abuse. The railway workers backed off and called on the sole policeman in the township to remove them. He put on his uniform, strapped on his handgun and went to the scene. When the Aboriginal men again refused to leave, he contacted the nearest station a couple of hundred kilometres away for assistance. The constable there responded immediately and set off, heavily armed. He stated at the subsequent hearing that he stopped on the way to test fire his weapons, anticipating conflict.

By the time he arrived, night had fallen and the men had long since dispersed to their homes. The two policemen drove into the area in an aggressive frame of mind and equipped with a shotgun and side-arms. A serious confrontation ensued, with the Aboriginal men using spears, boomerangs and nulla nullas (heavy clubs) and shots being fired by the police. Remarkably, no one was hurt on either side. The police retreated until assistance was provided some hours later by a contingent of armed officers from Alice Springs. They arrested the Aboriginal participants, who by that stage were asleep in their homes, and transported them to the Alice Springs Police Station. According to the men, they were taken separately from the cells, placed in a circle of police and severely beaten. Cyanide received special attention and, after being twice subjected to this treatment, was forced to mop up blood from the floor with his shirt.

I was staying with Geoff and his family when we were notified of the confrontation with the two police members by some

Finke community elders who, fearing further violence, had driven through the night for help. We contacted a local pilot and arrived in the township early on the following morning but, by then, the men had been taken into custody and were on their way to Alice Springs. It took some time to work out what had happened and the police station beatings had taken place before we arrived back and were able to see the arrested men.

I had been in Melbourne for some weeks when the charges against them were to come before the local court, and agreed to represent them. The hearing was conducted by the Chief Magistrate, who had come from Darwin. He accepted our contention that the whole incident had arisen because the Aboriginal men objected to the abusive racist manner in which they were treated by the railway workers, and rather than evidencing any respect for or recognition of their position, the police response aggravated the situation to the point where a dangerous confrontation developed. He was disturbed by the evidence relating to the events at the police station and said that, in his view, what had happened was indicative of an underlying problem that he had observed in Aboriginal and police relationships in the Northern Territory. His recommendation that a broad-based inquiry be conducted to address this issue was accepted by the Commonwealth Attorney-General, but after a change of government, it did not proceed. For the next ten years, I was seldom absent from Central or Northern Australia for more than two months.

An incident illustrates my perception at the time of the situation of the Aboriginal people in Central Australia. I was walking to the courthouse in Alice Springs, where my client would an hour or so later plead guilty to the manslaughter of another Aboriginal man who had been killed in a drunken brawl at a camp in the dry bed of the Todd River. As I passed the spot where it had occurred, I saw an almost identical fight was taking place. On this occasion, other men intervened and separated the combatants.

Later, at the court, when Justice Muirhead inquired as to whether my client intended to contest the charge, I responded he would plead guilty but that, apart from accepting legal responsibility and his sadness that he had killed a friend, I did not know what that really meant. Tragedies of this kind were the long-recognised predictable outcome of the social conditions in which Aboriginal people lived and for which, in large measure, our society was responsible. Yet only the accused, who was in more than one sense also a victim, would be held accountable. There was an inherent unfairness and societal hypocrisy in that approach. This was certainly understood by the judge who, in my experience, was a kindly person and always struggled with these issues.

In personal terms, my extended periods of absence from Victoria—altogether I spent about a third of my time away—were the source of much unhappiness. I disliked being away from Dawn and the children to the degree that I was. There was also a sense of unreality and disconnection about my life as I moved from the strange world of Owen Dixon Chambers—where the major concerns of the barristers during the 1970s appeared to relate to selecting the best tax minimisation techniques—to the impoverished Aboriginal communities of Central and Northern Australia.

Funding for the legal aid services in the Northern Territory was grossly inadequate and the fees paid barely covered my basic expenses. It would not have been possible for me to continue my involvement there without the support of some solicitor friends in Victoria who would make sure that there was work for me on my return home. So, I had little sympathy for my colleagues at the bar as they grappled with the problem of which scheme they should join to minimise the tax payable on their substantial incomes.

Despite the various difficulties, I really enjoyed my association with the Northern Territory. The intense colours of the country and the sky in Central Australia are indescribably beautiful. After rain, the seemingly barren red soil plains are covered with brilliantly coloured wild flowers and the suddenly flowing creeks fill with small fish that that have been waiting for this magical transformation. At night, stars cover the clear skies from horizon to horizon with occasional shooting stars or satellites passing overhead. I also enjoyed and was proud of my association with the many members of the Aboriginal community who were engaged in the struggle to improve the social conditions in which their people were living – and, course, the friendships that I developed with the other lawyers involved and the terrific and dedicated staffs at the health, education and legal services who were trying to assist, often in trying conditions and with minimal funding.

Once they were six years of age and accepted by the airlines as old enough to travel unaccompanied, the girls began to join me during school holidays. The first time was confusing for Kerry. She had travelled on her own, with a label pinned to her dress, and was collected at the airport by Geoff and some Aboriginal men who he was taking back to their settlement. I had been involved in an accident on the previous night when the car I was driving ran into some cattle on the highway, a couple of hundred kilometres away, and was still trying to get back. When we joined up, we set off for a two-day visit to a settlement for court hearings. Kerry was amazed that there were no street lights and at the sight of an Aboriginal group camped by the road side roasting a kangaroo in a fire. I declined the offer of barely singed meat on her behalf, but she had a great time. After we returned to Alice Springs, I spent hours trying to clean her clothes that were stained with red desert soil.

When I was in court, the girls were looked after by women at the Legal Aid Service, but at all other times, they stayed with me in a motel. They also came with me to several Aboriginal communities. We had some great trips together including one to Palm Valley, which is approximately 150 kilometres from Alice Springs. The last section of the journey was possible only in a four-wheel drive vehicle, and more difficult than I had expected. I became alarmed but they seemed to enjoy the bouncing around as we traversed the rough terrain. The valley contains a small area of trees that are vestiges of forests dating back to the time when Australia was part of the ancient continent of Gondwana. The girls were excited when we reached a large ancient meteorite crater and encountered a herd of wild horses. They were also taken at a separate time in a small plane to the Tiwi Islands settlements, which they loved.

The first indication that my daughters were destined for lives in the law appeared when they were still young and staying with me in Alice Springs. I had been briefed by another Legal Aid body to represent a prospector known locally as 'Russian Johnny'. As he was both Russian and used the anglicised name 'Johnny,' this was perhaps to be expected. He was charged with the murder of a car dealer who, with no commitment to honesty, advertised himself as 'Square Deal'. Johnny was on bail and saw us walking in the town centre. He told the girls he had some small pieces of gemstones he had found and wondered if they would like them. The girls were not sure about the morality of accepting a gift from a person who might be a murderer, and engaged in an analysis of the situation.

'Dad, Johnny didn't shoot Square Deal, did he?'

'Yes, he did.'

'But he didn't mean to?'

'Yes, he did.'

'He didn't intend to hurt him badly?'

'Yes, he did.'

'Did he do it to defend himself?'

'That's what he claims.'

'I believe him.'

They had worked their way through the elements of murder

and had arrived at a defence that enabled them to accept the pieces of gemstone. Johnny had a strong chance of acquittal, a view that was obviously held by the judge, but fearful of the prospect of many years in gaol, he accepted the prosecution offer of manslaughter. He received an effective sentence of three months' imprisonment. To the relief of the girls, this ensured his release before the following Christmas.

Some months later, I was walking along the main street in the town when I was approached by two huge and rough-looking men. One asked gruffly, 'You that Frank Vincent?' I was not at all sure that I wanted to acknowledge that or even that I knew this person but tentatively said, 'Yes.' He then smiled broadly and said, 'We want to shake your hand and buy you a beer. Johnny's a friend of ours.'

The girls were with me in the Northern Territory when a baby disappeared from a campsite at Uluru, and they followed the events carefully. Like many in the community, they regarded the apparent response and presentation of the child's mother, a woman named Lindy Chamberlain, as unusual. She claimed that her daughter had been taken by a native dog (a dingo), and they were inclined to disbelieve her.

This was a common and understandable response for two main reasons. First, although there were several later attacks, nothing of this kind had previously been reported and, second and much more importantly, the response of the child's mother was regarded as highly unusual. In order to make sense of our environment and how to function in it, we search for familiar explanations and expect people to react to events and circumstances in a conventional and predictable way and as we imagine we would ourselves. When their narratives are unusual or their conduct does not accord with our expectations, we doubt they are being truthful. Often this provides the basis upon which we make decisions.

Although we have lots of experience in assessing veracity from such signs in normal life, there is enormous potential for error. That is why the legal system has developed an elaborate set of evidentiary rules: they act as a filtering mechanism to limit this risk.

Their importance was not lost, many years later, on one of my grandsons, Jack. He was in fourth grade in primary school at the time of a conversation we had as I was taking him home one afternoon. The boys in his class traded football cards, and one of Jack's classmates had been caught stealing some from another boy. A couple of weeks later, the classmate was suspected of taking another valued card, and his album was checked. Nothing was found. When he told my grandson what had happened, his description suggested to Jack that the check had been incomplete.

This raised the question in my grandson's mind whether the boy was admitting the card would have been found if it had been done carefully.

'Poppa, why did he say they didn't look properly? Was he really saying that the card was there and that he was guilty?'

'He might have been, Jack. Sometimes people say and do things afterwards that show they know they are guilty.'

'You would have to be very careful as you might be wrong, Poppa, and that would be unfair.'

'That's what the High Court has decided, Jack.' Unlike much of the media coverage of the disappearance of the Chamberlain baby, Jack had appreciated the danger of inferring guilt too readily from post-event appearances or statements that might be perceived as self-incriminatory.

HOMICIDE

In Victoria, apart from some briefs in the Workers Compensation Board that I would pick up in the few days before and after each return home and that helped pay the bills, my work was almost exclusively confined to representing the defence in murder trials. Whether I was in Victoria or the Northern Territory, I felt surrounded by violence and wasted lives.

Homicide is seldom as it is portrayed on television or films. Generally, the circumstances are banal and frequently absurd. I have been involved in cases where the death of a person has been precipitated by the most trivial of matters, such as the purchase of a Christmas tree. In that case, it resulted from a drunken argument between the perpetrator and the victim about the respective merits of the plastic and real varieties. Another arose from the accidental shooting of a child, following the refusal of the accused's wife to delay going out until after she had made a cup of tea for him. He fired his rifle in anger with no intention of hurting her and hit the child of a neighbour. In one extraordinary case, the perpetrator stabbed his fiancée to death in a dispute over the design of their wedding invitations.

Sometimes the circumstances can almost defy belief. I handled a trial in Alice Springs where the death of an innocent but curious bystander came about because one three-year-old hit another at kindergarten. The events took place in an Aboriginal settlement. A number of men had returned from the town after a drinking bout lasting several days, and almost certainly still affected by alcohol. One of them was told by his wife that his child had been slapped by another during his absence. Incensed, he went to the home of the offending child and without discussion or warning punched the child's father, who fought back and forced him out of the house. Confused but now very angry, the innocent victim of this unprovoked attack then threw a heavy stone after him in the darkness. It missed his assailant but struck and killed a neighbour who had come from his own home, attracted by the commotion.

Not only did he have no idea why he had been attacked, he was also unaware of what had happened to his neighbour as he went to the attacker's home for some explanation. However, and without any explanation being provided, when he arrived, he was immediately subjected to a further assault by the attacker and his relatives, who beat him a second time. As he was walking back to his home, the unfortunate man encountered a group of people gathered about the fallen body of the neighbour. They beat him a third time. A little later, when he went to see the settlement nurse for treatment for the injuries he had sustained, he was attacked again – this time by the deceased's relatives. At no stage did he have any idea why these things were happening. Police arrived and he was charged with manslaughter and remanded in custody for several months before he was acquitted.

Commonly fuelled by alcohol, the death of a victim often results from the release of uncontrolled anger, the wellspring of which may not be recognised by the perpetrator. A number of the cases were the outcome of mental health issues, including some particularly sad matters where mothers suffering from puerperal syndrome killed their children.

Several seemed like the plots of poorly written, clichéd film scripts, particularly those involving the death of an unwanted husband or wife. Many attempted murder cases were of this kind.

Usually, the instigator—having watched too much television—had approached some individual in a hotel who they believed may have had criminal propensities or underworld contacts in search of a contract killer. They were almost always wrong in their assessment, and the police would be informed by an alarmed petty criminal who had no intention of being implicated. An undercover operative would be introduced to the instigator who, in due course, would be recorded seeking the death of the proposed victim. The operative would carefully draw their attention to the seriousness of the decision and the risks incurred. One clearly disenchanted former partner not only responded by repeatedly insisting, 'I want him dead', but demanded photographic proof of completion of the contract before making the final payment. Sometimes, it was only when the police informed the intended victims that they became aware of the extent of their relationship disharmony and that there was a plot to kill them.

Some of these plots, however, were successful, but those connected with them immediately came under suspicion. Apart from a small proportion of cases, murder is committed for one of a limited number of identifiable reasons and, in these situations represents the ultimate relationship breakdown. The possible motivations or the death and the likely perpetrators are often easily determined by experienced investigators.

In one such case, the police arranged through an intermediary for a female suspect and her lover to meet to discuss the progress of the investigation of her much older husband's death. Microphones were installed in the room and their arrangements with the drug addict they paid to carry out the killing were recorded. There was no indication that the victim ever suspected that his wife was unfaithful or that he was in jeopardy.

Another was reminiscent of the plot of the James M Cain novel, *The Postman Always Rings Twice*. The victim was a police sergeant stationed in a small country town when a newly joined member was sent to assist him. Very quickly, a sexual relationship developed between the sergeant's wife, who was unhappy in her marriage, and the young constable, whose own marriage had broken down. Afraid to confront him with their association, the young man chose the option of murder to resolve the problem. He decided to stage the killing in a way that would exclude himself from suspicion. The victim would be induced to go to an isolated location in the course of his duty where he would be shot by a criminal he was presumably endeavouring to apprehend.

The intended victim was at home, and the constable ostensibly in Melbourne, when he received a telephone call claiming that there was an apparently abandoned car on the side of a country road. When he went to check, out of the darkness emerged the young man crying and carrying a shotgun. He told the victim that he had been unable to go through with his plan. They returned to the station where they discussed the situation with the sergeant's wife.

It seemed that some kind of resolution was achieved, and the matter was not reported. Two to three weeks later, when the constable was supposed to be on leave in Melbourne, the sergeant received another call. He was told that there was an intruder stealing from a house under construction on the town outskirts. He went to the area where the constable was lying in wait. This time, the killer fired his shotgun, striking him in the stomach. Believing he had achieved his objective, he went to walk away when the fatally injured man fired at him with his service revolver while lying on the ground and hitting him several times in the back. The badly wounded killer was able to leave the scene but was soon found. One remarkable piece of evidence in the trial was that one of the victim's shots struck the killer's wrist, dislodging and damaging his watch and enabling a precise fixing of the time of the incident. The sergeant provided all the evidence necessary to convict the man who murdered him.

Among the worst cases I handled were those in which the victims were randomly selected for sexual or violent attack, mostly women, and those where very young children died at the hands of persons entrusted to care for them. Understandably, cases of these kinds resonate powerfully in our community as they strike at the heart of our sense of ourselves as human.

There were, of course, a number of tragic situations for which the criminal law was crude and inappropriate. In one such case where the jury formed the same view, my client was charged with the murder of her two children, one was aged three months and the other, two years. She had recognised that she was in a deeply disturbed mental state with suicidal thoughts following the recent birth and sought assistance from several sources, including her husband, her local doctor, a minister of religion and her relatives. Her concerns were dismissed on the basis that she was merely experiencing the 'baby blues' and that everything would be fine. Feeling totally unable to cope, after she broke down into uncontrollable weeping when she incorrectly labelled family Christmas presents, she decided to kill herself and the children. After drowning them in a bath, she tried to gas herself using her kitchen oven, slashed her wrists and ankles but was discovered near death and survived.

Under the law of Victoria, a woman who causes the death of an infant under the age of two years, while not having fully recovered from the effects of the child's birth, is regarded as guilty of infanticide. This is treated effectively as a form of manslaughter and does not necessitate imprisonment. In practice, it is rare for a gaol term to be imposed. However, the statute did not apply to the older child, where the likely verdicts were either guilty of murder or not guilty on the ground of insanity: the latter attracting an order of indefinite detention.

There is no justification for the distinction in a case where the deaths result from the same mental illness, but it created a serious problem for the defence. Whether what seemed to me to be a just outcome could be achieved would depend entirely upon the jury's view of the situation. Fortunately, the trial judge permitted considerable latitude in the presentation of the defence case, even allowing me to be with my client in the dock and holding her while she made a statement to the jury.

By the time they retired to consider their verdict, I was emotionally exhausted and sat by myself on a bench in a park opposite the court as I awaited the result. They saw no justice in her conviction and returned with verdicts of not guilty. Before I left the court, I made sure that arrangements were put in place for her continuing care.

Often after difficult or demanding trials, barristers practising in the area could be found at a particular table in a coffee shop in the Owen Dixon Chambers building. There was usually someone there, and we provided support for each other. On this occasion, however, the trial was held in the country, and as soon as I returned to Melbourne, I caught a plane to Canberra where I was to appear in a case on the following day before the High Court.

The matter raised complex issues of law relating to the interaction of Commonwealth and State Government powers under our federal structure. After I checked into a hotel, I tried to settle down and work on my brief, but it was hopeless. I took a beer from the minibar and sat in bed watching a late-night movie on the television. On arrival at the court on the next morning, feeling inadequately prepared, I was extremely concerned. Miraculously, it transpired that the issue at the centre of my case had arisen in another matter only two days earlier, and the judges did not consider that they needed to hear any further argument on it. I could not believe my good luck but disingenuously expressed my deep disappointment.

Another of my clients, who was also in a state of deep depression when she strangled her two children with a skipping rope, was found not guilty on the ground of insanity. She had broken down following breast augmentation surgery undertaken to please her husband, at his urging, that resulted in disfigurement and continuing pain. She decided to kill herself but was fearful of what would happen to the children when she was no longer able to care for them. Her own childhood experience had been one of extreme loneliness and isolation from her family in boarding schools. In her disordered mind, she concluded that they should die together. After she killed them, she dressed them in their pyjamas and placed them in their beds. When her husband arrived home, he found her, dissociated from reality, checking their school homework.

Generally, the motivations of those who kill or cause injury to others, and who are not severely mentally ill or involved in criminal enterprise, tend to be related to basic human emotions and there are few, if any, who can be reasonably described as 'winners'. In domestic violence situations, it seemed to me that the perpetrators (almost always males) had reverted to a childlike state in which they saw themselves as the true victims. They appeared to have reasoned, 'I will kill you, and then you will understand and be sorry for what you have done to me', without any real appreciation of the significance of their decision, even for themselves.

This response is usually described as a desire for revenge, and sometimes that is an adequate explanation, but the position is often more complex. As I see it, many respond to behaviour that so powerfully impacts upon their sense of self that they feel that equilibrium can only be restored by a primitive striking out, usually against the person regarded as responsible. The simplification of complex motivation into notions of power and revenge can have particularly unfortunate consequences in addressing the issues of domestic violence because it emphasises the outcome rather than its origins, which are deep seated in our cultures and manifested in almost every aspect of our personal and social relationships.

Among the objects and methods employed to cause death that I encountered in my work were firearms of various kinds, knives and other objects used for stabbing or cutting, axes, hammers, clubs, a variety of cords for strangulation, motor vehicles, poisons, setting fires, drowning, the injection of battery acid, strangulation and even hurling the victim from the upper floor of a high-rise building. I certainly do not want to dwell upon the measures adopted or the various motives and circumstances under which lives were taken, still less on the means chosen to dispose of the bodies.

Careful preparation for these trials was essential and involved examination of crime scenes where possible. I tried to visit them, if possible, at times and under conditions approximating to those existing when the events occurred. Once, I was bailed up by armed police who had been alerted by the nervous staff of a bank where an armed robbery had taken place as I was looking around a lane at the rear of the premises. On another such visit, I went to a recessed area in a darkened lane at about two o'clock in the morning where a victim had been stabbed and left to die. It was located in an industrial area and surrounded by old factories, and I was satisfied that it must have been deliberately chosen. In daylight, the lane would not have suggested menace but at that hour, there could be little doubt.

Where possible, I endeavoured to have my client's case supported by detailed forensic investigation. Sometimes, this was of great assistance and, in one case, crucial. My client was aged nineteen years when he was charged with the murder of a woman who was walking across a public park in broad daylight with her child who she had just picked up from kindergarten. She had been hit twice by bullets fired, the media initially reported, by a sniper. It did not take long for the police to identify the position from which the shots had been fired, to find the rifle which was equipped with a telescopic sight and to interview the young man responsible. He was adamant that the rifle was accidentally discharged only once and that there was no magazine in the weapon at the time. This was clearly not correct and, from the police perspective, the case they were dealing with, a thrill killing by a seriously disturbed young man, seemed so strong that they gave little regard to any other possibility.

When I saw him, he asserted that, as soon as he realised he had shot the victim (but unaware she had been hit twice) he sought the advice of a teenage friend who suggested the story of accidental discharge. He said he had been firing at signs and posts on the park boundary and simply had not seen her.

I went to the park with my school-age daughters on the following weekend and we examined the boundary looking for bullet holes. There were plenty and they had a common characteristic: almost all were significantly to the right of a post or sign. Only a very few had struck what appeared as the intended target. It seemed there was a distinct possibility that he may have been telling the truth. Arrangements were made through the Public Solicitor to test this. First, the rifle was examined and shown to deflect bullets to the right, while the telescopic sight was a cheap model with a limited arc of vision and some looseness in the lenses that created the possibility of an additional measurable deviation. A meteorologist estimated the wind speed and direction across the park at the time of the incident and its possible effect on the trajectory of a bullet discharged from that rifle. His report also supported the young man's assertion. The area was carefully mapped and distances accurately measured.

A probabilities calculation indicated that there was only a five per cent chance that the unfortunate woman was within the field of vision at the time that rifle was discharged. Diagrams were then prepared setting out the accumulated information for presentation to the jury in the trial. The young man was acquitted of murder but found guilty of manslaughter through his commission of an unlawful and dangerous act.

RECONCILIATION

Although Dawn and I were living apart, we were never truly separated. Throughout the entire period, we were in constant contact and always cooperated to ensure a stable and normal environment for our girls. They continued to live in the family home, did not change schools, and there was never any issue between us concerning access. We had joint birthday parties for them and took them on holidays together. Sometimes when I was away, Dawn and the children stayed in my flat in Armadale as she felt more secure there.

We spent one extremely hot January with the children, visiting Aboriginal groups on cattle stations and small settlements. The purpose was to gather information for a submission to the Australian Law Reform Commission on the incorporation of Aboriginal customary law in our system of justice. Unable to secure funding for the project, we had decided to use the holiday period. Dawn spoke with the women while I met with the men. She obtained a much more honest picture than I did of the prevalence of sexual and physical violence in the various communities and the extent to which women and children lived in fear.

As part of this endeavour, we visited a settlement on a cattle station to the north west of Alice Springs, arriving at the camp after a long, hot journey along a dusty, rough track. I spoke with the men, who described a community of almost idyllic social harmony, while Dawn met with the women some distance away. The girls were tired and irritable and, when they started to argue over a can of soft drink, she lost patience with them, much to the amusement of the Aboriginal women, who then relaxed. She obtained a much more reliable and honest description than I did of the real situation. In common with all the other places we visited, they reported endemic sexual and domestic abuse and violence. We went to another where the local men objected to Dawn meeting with the women. However, she was able to discuss the situation with a number at the community health centre and found that it was no different.

It was a great time in other respects, with some memorable family experiences. Most nights we camped under the stars, but on one occasion, we slept in an empty house, which we discovered was infested with dangerous spiders. At another settlement, the girls proudly displayed a large snake they had watched the Aboriginal children kill. When Dawn asked me about it, I did not tell her that it was a taipan, one of the world's most venomous reptiles. On that trip, the Legal Aid field officer with us was disappointed when he demonstrated his prowess with a new expensive rifle he had purchased, only to have Dawn, who had never previously fired one, outshoot him. I was a hopeless third and did not hit the drink can targets once.

Our findings were reported to Law Reform Commission but I was never further contacted about them. It is deeply regrettable that, although what was happening was widely known for a long time, little attention was given to the problems within those communities until almost thirty years later. The primary reasons for this delay were, I believe, that to deal with them would have required public recognition of the situation in which our Indigenous community has been placed as a result of more than two hundred years of racial discrimination. A major consequence of the generational adoption of damaging policies has been the creation of generations of damaged people and communities. Healing is not easily achieved and requires genuine commitment to work with and support them in their endeavours over a long period. Just as the damage has been generational, so, unfortunately, can be the repair.

Dawn and I continued to meet for dinner, but the evenings could be tense, and we argued in some of Melbourne's best restaurants. On one occasion, I was working in Alice Springs when I rang her. The trial I was engaged in was expected to finish within the week, so we arranged to meet on the following Saturday night. Unfortunately, it proceeded a little more slowly. Rather than postpone our dinner for a few days, I booked a flight for the Saturday morning to return on the following day, made a restaurant reservation and bought a new outfit from Alice Springs' 'finest' clothing store. We had another restaurant argument, and altogether it was an expensive disaster.

From early 1975 to my appointment to the Supreme Court in April 1985, I would typically be in Central and Northern Australia for three weeks at a time, usually starting with a homicide case, and then appearing in the Court of Summary Jurisdiction in Alice Springs, Tennant Creek and Aboriginal settlements as well as the Children's Court. Back in Victoria, the work in murder trials was virtually continuous. During one particular month, I acted for the defence in four trials in succession before the same judge. Twice, the next trial started while the jury in the previous one was deliberating. This was possible as they were generally much shorter than they would later become, and because of the approach I adopted.

As I mentioned earlier, the elements of the crime of murder are relatively straightforward, and the practical issues of proof are usually narrowly confined. The jury address constitutes the culmination and last opportunity to present the defence. Sometimes, it may have to resonate for many days after it has been delivered and survive the dispassionate identification of the issues in the judge's charge. While a powerful performance may appear impressive and have temporary emotional impact, this must be expected to dissipate quickly once the jury commences their deliberation and concentrates on the detail of the evidence and the arguments presented.

My objective was to ensure the perspective from which I wanted them to approach the issues and the evidence remained in the forefront of their minds, and the various techniques adopted in my addresses were directed to that end. This did not mean that the expression of emotion had no part to play, but care had to be taken. The perception by jurors of falsity or inappropriate theatricality at this level could damage my credibility and through me that of the defence. I found the more conversational approach I had learned to employ in courts in Central Australia, where it was necessary to dispel their reservations about the 'lawyers from the south' was very useful in this respect.

The pressure of this workload was enormous, and I pushed myself to extreme limits, handling twenty or so murder cases per year. During one busy period, I had been appearing in a trial in Melbourne, which finished on a Friday night, and left for Darwin on the next morning. After conferring with the client in Berrimah Prison on the Sunday, I started another on the Monday, which lasted a week. I then flew to Alice Springs and started a third on the following Tuesday.

As funding for the Legal Aid Service was limited, I was accommodated in a fairly basic hostel that housed the railway track workers engaged in the maintenance of the line from Adelaide. After being awakened by the noise as they were setting off at six o'clock, I decided to do some work before we resumed. By that evening, as I sat in the Adelaide airport lounge for about twenty minutes while waiting to board the Melbourne flight for home, I was so exhausted that I fell asleep. The next thing I remember is being shaken awake by a cleaner, hours later. The airport was closed for the night, and I went to a hotel in the city.

I tried to harden myself to the terrible situations and people

I had to deal with, and mostly succeeded. Sometimes, when this did not work, it became necessary to carefully conceal my personal reactions. This is a common and sometimes unavoidable experience for criminal lawyers acting within a legal system based on the rule of law under which any charged individual is entitled to the presumption of innocence and a proper defence at their trial. Despite the pressures involved, I was attracted to the work and had no interest in the much less demanding and considerably more lucrative role of arguing about other people's money.

My life continued in this fashion until early 1979 when three Aboriginal children together with an intellectually disabled nineteen-year-old and an older female were charged with the murder of the owner of an isolated cattle station called Huckitta, north east of Alice Springs. He had been shot with his own rifle by a twelve-year-old boy who, with the other accused, had stolen a car and run off from the settlement in which they lived. My client was a thirteen-year-old girl. The trial was expected to take three weeks, but we were there for over three months. I was able to return to Melbourne for only one weekend during that period. Most of the hearing was occupied with argument about the admissibility of evidence of admissions obtained from our clients, which, it was clear, had been obtained in blatant disregard of their ages and rights.

We were unsuccessful in our defence, and the young people were sent to adult gaol. Our subsequent appeals eventually reached the High Court and were also unsuccessful, but the principles for which we contended relating to the abuse of police power were recognised and adopted just two years later and have been applied many times since.

An event during that trial has remained a powerful memory for me. It occurred on my client's fourteenth birthday. She was wearing a light cardigan I had bought her as a present and was about to read a prepared statement from the court dock. To keep it safe, she had carried it in her shoe which she removed. She unfolded this piece of paper and read laboriously. It was a terribly sad scene, particularly as she had had little, if any, real involvement in the death.

Towards the end of the trial, Dawn and I decided to meet in Surfers Paradise for a week's holiday. For practical purposes, we were back together, although I was still living in the flat. I then received a call from Legal Aid in Melbourne inquiring about my availability to appear for a well-known criminal, Ray Bennett, the leader of a group of three charged with the machine gun murder of an equally notorious criminal underworld individual, Leslie Kane. I declined, pointing out I had been absent from home for almost three months, and my wife and I were going to have a short break before I resumed work. Bennett responded that he wanted me to represent him and would be happy to have a junior counsel prepare his case at my direction if I conducted his defence at trial. When it was made clear to him that I would not be able to meet with him until the day before the trial commenced, he said that would be fine. Legal Aid approved this unusual arrangement, and the brief was sent to me at Surfers Paradise. I worked on it by the hotel pool and gave directions to my junior counsel and solicitor by phone.

It was a strange case. The prosecution claimed that the shooting had occurred in the bathroom of a unit occupied by Kane and his wife, and that the weapon used was a rifle that had been modified to operate as a machine gun. Not only was that an unlikely scenario, there being no damage whatsoever to the bathroom (which meant every shot would have had to strike and remain within the victim's body) and there were no blood traces or other forensic evidence of any kind to suggest anything untoward had happened. No body had been found, and Kane's large pink car was never located.

I was also intrigued by the fact that there was no evidence that he was alive on the day the killing was claimed to have taken place, and became convinced that whatever may have happened had occurred at least a day or two earlier and certainly not in the way the prosecution contended. The shooting was not reported to the police for more than twenty-four hours after it had allegedly occurred, and the three men accused all had sound, and as far I could judge, genuine alibis for the time claimed.

It was also troubling that when I sought access to the recordings of the initial police interview with Kane's widow, who asserted she had witnessed her husband's death, I was informed that one of them had been 'lost'. We were able to demonstrate the prosecution case rested on dubious and incomplete evidence and was seriously suspect. That Kane had been killed seemed to be beyond doubt—he was never seen or heard from again, but what happened has never been revealed.

Although we were successful in his defence, my client benefited little: he was shot dead by a gunman in a court building only a few weeks later and in circumstances that also gave rise to a number of still unanswered and disturbing questions. He had been charged with involvement in some unrelated armed robberies and was being escorted to a courtroom by two unarmed police members for a preliminary hearing when a man, seated in a corridor along which he had to pass, suddenly stepped in front of them and shot him at close range. In a well-planned and audacious execution, the gunman escaped through a side door that led to a police garage area adjoining the court building and then through a small gap in the surrounding fence at the rear where cars were parked. Even though the shooting occurred in a court building and the gunman must have been seen by many people, he was never identified. Another of the three men who had faced the court in the trial disappeared, presumed dead, at around the same time, while the third decamped for parts unknown.

I was still living in the flat in Armadale but by this time, it was essentially being used as a second family home. While the arrangement had some advantages in view of the type of work in which I was engaged, I was happy when, a few months later, I returned to live with Dawn and the children. From what I have heard about the experiences of others, our period apart had been unusual in many respects. We never argued about money or our children: money because it was not considered important, and our children because they were. We had survived as a powerfully united couple. Of course, there were many challenges in store for us, but nothing ever threatened to separate us again, and we entered a new stage in our lives.

Dawn had commenced working as a social worker at the Commonwealth Rehabilitation Service. She enjoyed her time there as the centre where she was working provided a range of integrated services, delivered through multidisciplinary teams, for people with mental and physical impairments. The later abandonment of this model, which rested on a broad view of rehabilitation, in favour of employment directed programs was regrettable and reflected the continuing approach of government and industry that we both rejected of regarding human beings primarily in terms of their perceived economic value. She has continued to work in the field of mental health rehabilitation and counselling since that time and maintained her links with her former workmates.

By this time, I was frequently provided with the assistance of junior counsel, who relieved me of some of the pressure of an absurdly heavy workload. This was effectively formalised when my application for appointment as Queen's Counsel was successful at the end of 1980.

My work remained generally the same but with possibly a larger proportion of even more difficult cases and terrible crimes. Among the worst of them, although it seems absurd to even attempt to make such a comparison, was the trial of a man named Harding, who asserted his innocence of the rape and murder of a four-year-old

Vietnamese girl in the block of public housing flats where he was employed as a maintenance worker. The case against him was strong and the circumstances dreadful, but he was entitled to have his defence properly presented. My junior counsel described our role as similar to that of two workers with shovels who attempt to clean out a nauseating pit each day, only to have it refilled to a higher level each night.

Another, which emphasised the particular vulnerability of women in our community to random selection for violent sexual attack, involved a teenage girl who was forced at gunpoint to enter the killer's car. She was walking at around noon on a bright sunny day along a main street when he stopped beside her. He had a few hours earlier had an argument with his girlfriend and was driving around filled with anger when he saw this girl. She was taken to an isolated location, raped and killed by a shotgun blast directly into her face. Still not satisfied, he returned to the same area where he was intercepted by the police. Although many years have passed, I can still see her.

It is not always easy for the community, and particularly for those directly affected by criminal behaviour, or the lawyers themselves to accept their role in cases of this kind. However, it is fundamentally important that this is done if the rule of law is to be genuinely maintained in our society. This is why the bar has traditionally operated on a 'cab rank' principle, under which it is normally regarded as a breach of ethics to refuse a brief in an area of law where the barrister practises. There were certainly times when I would much have preferred to be prosecuting rather than defending my client.

One unusual process I became involved in towards the end of my time as a barrister concerned a man named Knowles. He had been convicted of murder some six years earlier and continued to insist that he was innocent. Finally, while it was thought unlikely anything would come of it, the Public Solicitor agreed to secure an independent assessment of his trial and conviction, and I was engaged for this purpose.

A review of the transcript left me with the impression of inadequate preparation of the defence case and, in particular, raised questions in my mind relating to some evidence that had not been brought to the jury's attention. Knowles had contended that the female deceased, who he had met at a singles group on or before the night of her death and with whom he thought he was getting on well, inexplicably became violent and attacked him with a knife. In the ensuing struggle, she was accidentally killed. Apart from its inherent improbability, there were two major difficulties with this story: first, there was evidence presented by a forensic pathologist, called by the prosecution, that he had identified two separate stab wounds and, second, the fact that Knowles had disguised himself and hidden for the following two years. He claimed that he had panicked, believing that his seemingly extraordinary version would not be accepted.

I was informed that there was a former South Australian homicide detective who claimed to have informed the defence before the trial that he had earlier been in a relationship with the deceased and that she was, in fact, prone to irrational violent outbursts. The lawyers acting at that time denied having received any such information until much later and asserted that, in any event, they did not consider that it would have been admissible in the trial. When I interviewed him, the man seemed credible and provided similar descriptions of the deceased's behaviour to that given by Knowles and continued to claim he had informed the defence lawyers prior to the trial.

It occurred to me that, if Knowles and this man were telling the truth, there might be other evidence available. In response to my inquiry about this possibility, he mentioned that the woman had been previously married and her former husband was still living in South Australia. When this person, in turn, was contacted, he was understandably reluctant to become involved and referred us to the divorce records in the Supreme Court in Melbourne. Examination of his initiating Petition, filed some years before the woman's death, disclosed assertions of repeated conduct of a similar kind.

This was completely independent evidence that existed well before the events we were concerned with and about which Knowles knew nothing. It provided compelling support for the possibility of his version being truthful. Further consideration of the pathologist's evidence revealed that his finding of two knife wounds was almost certainly erroneous. The unreliability of that witness' evidence generally became apparent in several subsequent cases.

Knowles had previously appealed unsuccessfully against his conviction and so the only available avenue open was to seek the reconsideration of the case by the Governor in Council through a Petition of Mercy. This was initially rejected but after further representations was referred to the Supreme Court.

By the time that the case was heard, I had been engaged by the Commonwealth Special Minister of State to conduct an Inquiry into possible corruption within the publicly owned telecommunications company, Telecom, and Knowles was represented by other counsel. The conviction was overturned, and a retrial ordered. When he was then given the opportunity to plead guilty to manslaughter, Knowles accepted, saying he had no faith in the system. Having already served more than seven years imprisonment, he was released immediately. But he had little opportunity to enjoy his freedom and died from a heart attack, several months later.

In view of the cost to the Legal Aid services of a rule at the time under which a QC could only appear with a junior barrister, who would have to receive a fee equivalent to two-thirds of an appropriate senior's fee, initially I did not apply for appointment in the Northern Territory. However, I did so after I was approached by Chief Justice Forster, who, to enable me to continue my work with the legal services, arranged for the rule to be waived in cases where I represented Aboriginal accused.

My last appearance in the Northern Territory was made in the Children's Court at Yuendemu, a settlement approximately three hundred kilometres west of Alice Springs, in April 1985, following another murder trial in Darwin. The sitting occupied three days, and most of my young clients were charged with theft or the illegal use of motor cars. It was difficult to get much sense out of them as they were badly affected by chronic petrol sniffing which was endemic in the area and resulted in permanent brain damage for many young people. Rather than ordering their detention in Alice Springs, the Magistrate released those who were found guilty into the custody of the community elders to be taken to bush camps, in the hope that they could be helped by cultural training as the best of a very limited range of options available to him.

Unknown to me at the time, the murder trial that commenced about ten days after I arrived back in Victoria would be my last. It was a relatively straightforward case of self-defence arising from a brawl in a hotel on the outskirts of Melbourne. The jury was taken for a view of the location and gained insight when a drunken man almost started another brawl when he harassed one of the female court shorthand reporters. My client was quickly acquitted.

When my appointment was announced, the lawyers at the Aboriginal Legal Aid Service in Alice Springs commissioned a traditional painting by a well-known local artist that was to be presented to me as an expression of appreciation for my work in Central Australia. Sadly, it was destroyed when disgruntled teenagers burned down the office. I never saw it.

THE SUPREME COURT

I was at home watching television with Dawn and the girls, in late April 1985, when I received an unexpected phone call from the Victorian Attorney-General. He said that one of the Supreme Court judges was ill and another was soon to retire. At the request of the Chief Justice, a replacement was to be appointed early, and he offered me the position, which I accepted. When I returned and told Dawn and the girls, Lisa, who was thirteen at the time, gave me a guiding principle for the new role to which I hope I always adhered: 'Always remember that your decisions affect real people'.

I was enthusiastic about the new position. A Supreme Court appointment represented a remarkable level of personal and professional success, and I was honoured to have the opportunity. Later, I was often asked whether I missed the bar and could truthfully answer 'no'. There was no realistic prospect of continuing indefinitely to subject myself to the stresses of a seemingly endless series of murder trials that had become an almost normal state of affairs for me even if I had wanted to do so, and I certainly did not. I had no particular interest in any other area of the law or desire to embark on building a new practice. I felt like a boxer who, after many bouts, was immensely relieved that he never had to enter the ring again.

My first case was a sentencing hearing, where the accused, who was charged with the attempted murder of his wife, pleaded guilty to the much less serious offence of unlawful wounding. He had stabbed her in the arm during a domestic dispute. Precisely how the confrontation developed was unclear, and the head injuries he had sustained from blows from a tomahawk wielded by her were much more severe and required hospitalisation for several weeks. Both claimed to have acted in self-defence, and, based on the material available to me, either version could have been true. There was nothing in the history of the matter or the backgrounds of the parties to indicate why the police had decided to proceed against the accused rather than his wife and, importantly, no evidence of prior violence or abuse. Unless something emerged during the hearing, it was, I thought, after reading the evidence, almost certain that I would not sentence him to imprisonment.

I was listening attentively to the submissions of his barrister when the prosecutor, my friend Fred James, interrupted. Somehow, in my endeavour to ensure that I had not overlooked anything, I had created the impression in his mind that I was contemplating sending the man to gaol. Fred thought that would be a terrible result and intervened to indicate the prosecution's support for the defence contentions. I assured everyone that I had not been carried away by my newly acquired status, and an order was made.

There was much to learn about my new job, as I soon discovered. The Chief Justice, who was firmly of the view there should be no specialist judges, informed me that I would be allocated mainly to civil cases for some time. This required me to familiarise myself with areas I had never practised in and about which I hadn't the slightest interest. I frequently cursed him—silently during the day and noisily at home—for the first few years. Nevertheless, his approach required me to acquire a much better understanding of the multifaceted nature of our legal system and the way its underlying objectives and values were reflected in diverse and seemingly unconnected areas. It was almost twenty years before a separate criminal division of the Supreme Court was established. I understand why this became necessary, but, as is often the case with increased specialisation, the possession of this broad experience among judges has been reduced.

The assumption is made in relation to judicial appointments that demonstrated competence as a practising lawyer or recognised academic attainment sufficiently qualifies an individual for the role. I soon learned that more was required. Judges are almost always successful legal practitioners or highly respected academics, but it does not follow that they possess any special insights when dealing with human behaviours or motivations or are temperamentally suited for the role. Some of the worst judges I have appeared before, or encountered while on the bench, were blinded by their self-image and sublime confidence in the correctness of their views.

Decision-making in the legal process is not, and cannot be, mechanical. The law itself usually requires the balancing of interests and values, and there are almost always contested facts and conclusions that are dependent on the perceived credibility and reliability of witnesses. However much they may pretend and present themselves as totally objective in their approach and assessments, judges bring their personal experiences and values with them to these tasks. Judging is a human process and those entrusted with this responsibility will not only inevitably reflect the times and values of the community that they represent but are appointed to do so.

The real challenges of the role related to the development of insight into the factors that may be influencing my assessments of the relative importance of the various considerations raised in the case, whether in balancing interests or fact finding. This required an honest exploration of my views, perspectives and possible sources of prejudice that I had not previously been required to undertake. Obviously, advocates have to identify the issues involved in a dispute and understand the position being advanced by their opponents. However, as representatives of the parties that engage them, their role generally does not require balancing respective interests but rather advancing those of their clients.

The transition to the bench also required me to gain not only substantial understanding of parts of the law of which I had been happily ignorant but a new skill—judgement writing. The work of a judge in the Supreme Court involved a massive amount of writing at night and weekends, and I found this demanding, particularly when I was not confident about my understanding of the law in an unfamiliar area.

There was also an issue of credibility for some time with practitioners in the civil area. More than a few had understandable doubts about the ability of this new judge, who was identified as a criminal lawyer, to deal with the complex issues that sometimes had to be decided. To equip myself to handle these cases, I undertook as much research as I could before each matter. As I earlier mentioned, there are common threads of principles and values that underpin almost all of the elements of the legal system, with adaptations designed to deal with the problems and requirements of particular kinds of disputes, so it was not as difficult as I feared to deal with them. I soon became accustomed to the role and began to enjoy the research and the challenges presented in the different areas.

My confidence was boosted substantially not long after my appointment when I gave judgement in a case involving a technically difficult area of civil law. The judgement was researched and written over a weekend, then handed down on the following Monday morning. I hoped that I was right but, as my father would have said, thought that it was 'even money each of two' (equally possible) that I had missed some important consideration or legal principle and was hopelessly wrong. Some days later, I was approached by the court librarian who told me that the judgement was in great demand by practitioners. It was sent for inclusion in the law reports and, for years afterwards, was a standard resource in similar cases.

The Supreme Court has changed dramatically since my appointment. There were no female judges then, and within days of taking the position, several of my new colleagues urged me not to engage a female associate. One was adamant that a judge should not be alone with his associate for lengthy periods, particularly on circuit. I was uncertain whether he was worried about my possible lapse into temptation or his own. Another regarded it as inappropriate because, he assured me, 'women can't drink' and were therefore unsatisfactory companions. A third adopted a curious and rather amusing compromise. He did engage a female associate, but she was not permitted to accompany him on circuit or to be in the court building after sunset. I do not know what he feared might happen once the sun went down.

Women lawyers were expected to wear skirts in court, provided, of course that, in the judge's view, they were not too short. There was no agreement as to how this was assessed. Pantsuits were frowned upon. A male barrister was criticised because he was wearing a striped shirt under his gown. It was all very silly.

There were some remarkable conventions followed. Some were merely quaint and mildly amusing, but I was very uncomfortable with others. For example, if a judge was encountered walking along a court corridor, staff members were required to stand back against the wall until the august being passed by. In proceeding down the staircases behind courtrooms, associates were expected to walk in front of their judges and behind when they returned, in case the judge slipped. When it was pointed out by one of my fellow judges that I had breached this particular convention, I responded that I was capable of safely proceeding up and down a few stairs and that under no circumstances would I fall on my associate, male or female.

At judges' meetings, we were seated in strict order of seniority, with the most junior judge at the bottom of the long table. I complained to other members that I was so far away that I could barely see the Chief Justice due to the earth's curvature. Initially, the junior judge was responsible for keeping the minutes. These would then be approved by the Chief Justice and any sign of disagreement or possibly controversial comment removed before distribution. I disliked these meetings intensely and avoided attendance when possible. After I was appointed to the Adult Parole Board, this became relatively easy as I was able to schedule meetings to coincide with those being held in the Court. The task of minute secretary was then given to the Chief Justice's associate.

The older members were welcoming and approachable if I needed assistance, but their perspectives on many matters differed significantly from mine, particularly on those they perceived as affecting their role and status. More than once, my contributions to discussion on issues with this potential were met with silence as if I had not spoken.

Another of the more recently appointed judges and I were embarrassed that there were no women members of either the Supreme Court or the County Court, and proposed at one of the meetings that, at least, the formal mode of address of 'Mr Justice' should be changed to 'Justice'. This was hardly revolutionary and was intended simply to indicate openness but was overwhelmingly rejected. Several of us dropped the 'Mr' anyhow, and it was not long before it disappeared.

The welcome dinner held by the Court on appointment would be attended only by the judges and held at one of two conservative clubs. This ceased at the time of my appointment due to increasing concern about the restrictive membership practices of both. Wives (no other partners were recognised) were invited to farewell dinners, when, it was said, their husbands were handed back.

The judges were, without exception, incredibly intelligent and hardworking. A number were ex-servicemen who had been in combat during the Second World War, and they brought to the role a special level of personal experience and human insight that I greatly respected. There was also a strange, almost monastic commitment by my colleagues to their role that would never be accepted now.

A new judge could certainly call upon more experienced members for advice, but most were usually busy working on their own legally and factually complex matters. Consequently, we tended to work in isolation from each other with limited discussion of any of the issues with which we were grappling.

It was also expected that, if the case listed before him did not proceed for some reason, the judge would indicate his availability to hear any other matter in the list. On circuit, if no Supreme Court cases were ready to proceed, they would hear County Court matters. This also occurred from time to time in the city. As a barrister, I sometimes found on arriving at the County Court that my case had been transferred. Although it was done to increase efficiency and reduce waiting times, the clients would be terrified, thinking—with some justification—that, if convicted, they could expect a longer sentence in the higher jurisdiction.

There were no arrangements for judgement writing, which was done at night or during weekends. In common with my colleagues, I also worked on drafts during holiday periods. To avoid the build-up of outstanding cases, judgements would be given orally and immediately when possible. This was very important in relation to rulings made in the course of a civil or criminal trial. When doing this, I would indicate to counsel that my reasons would be provided within a few days and in a 'more comprehensible form of the English language,' so that, if necessary, any mistake or oversight could be addressed.

There was no separate Court of Appeal for the first ten years after my appointment, and all judges were allocated to this work from time to time. Generally, this would increase with seniority and experience. In my case, however, some interpersonal relationship issues within the Court resulted in much more frequent allocation. I never knew why, but two very senior judges refused to sit with or even speak to each other in any circumstances. Criminal and civil appeal cases were heard by three judges, and it was sometimes difficult to find enough who were not in dispute to constitute a bench. I was not involved in any of these internal arguments and found myself sitting in both civil and criminal appeals within a few months of commencing. This afforded me a remarkable opportunity to engage in and increase my understanding of all aspects of the Court's work.

Usually when dealing with an appeal, one judge would prepare a draft for discussion and, hopefully, agreement or modification. I was sitting with the Chief Justice and another senior judge when I prepared my first. Eager to demonstrate I was up to the task, I put a tremendous amount of effort into it before I finally sent it to them. Some days later, the Chief Justice's copy appeared on my desk with only one comment. He pointed out a minor grammatical error on one page: a split infinitive. I took that as indicating agreement.

Generally, in the many different areas that I was required to address, I found the work absorbing, and there were always new challenges. A piece of advice given to me by a former Court member proved invaluable in this regard. He said, 'When presented with something new, I say as little as I can for as long as I can in the hope that either the barristers will sort it out themselves, which they usually do, or that they will say enough to enable me to eventually work my way through it. If that doesn't work, I adjourn to find the answer.' He was a great judge, and I suspect he rarely found himself in that predicament.

The first major criminal trial I presided over was the trial of the four men charged with involvement in the detonation of a bomb outside the police headquarters in Russell Street, Melbourne, in March 1986. A young policewoman was killed and some other people were severely injured, including a police member who was shot while arresting one of the suspects. As I mentioned earlier, it was intended by the Chief Justice that I would be allocated primarily to civil cases for some time, but this was treated as an exception because of my experience as counsel in substantial criminal trials. Altogether, the proceedings occupied around six months. The preparation of rulings and jury instructions, as issues arose, and my final charge, required constant attention so I had only a few evenings and no weekends free for the entire period.

Due to its serious nature and potential consequences, involvement in a criminal trial is almost always stressful for all concerned with the process. Some, like that of a man named Leslie Camilleri, who, with co-offender Lindsay Beckett, was guilty of the murder of two teenage girls abducted from a country town in New South Wales and then repeatedly sexually assaulted before they were brutally killed, can be extremely distressing and remain so for me, even after many years. The unemotional manner of Beckett, who gave evidence in the trial, was chilling. The horrified silence in which it was received by those present was broken only by an occasional sound of intense pain from one or other of the girls' mothers. I will never forget it.

Although the trials of Camilleri and Beckett were among the worst in this sense that I presided over, there were others that, in their separate circumstances, were almost as, if not equally, horrific. Even to refer to them, as I have done here, evokes memories and feelings I prefer to avoid. I had to deal with many cases involving appalling behaviour and terrible human consequences in my various roles as barrister, judge and parole board chair, and generally managed to cope fairly well in compartmentalising them. When this did not happen, and it was not always possible to identify the trigger or guard against it, my major objective was to maintain control of my responses and not let them affect my performance or my external life and relationships.

Judges have the responsibility of doing their best to ensure a fair trial can be seen to be had. They must therefore be careful to control their own natural reactions to the evidence or individuals involved. To do this is vitally important, but maintaining a stance of judicial calm for extended periods can be difficult. In common with many occupations in our society, only during the last few years has there been any recognition of the stress inherent in the role of barrister or judge and any attempt made to provide personal support.

The stress was experienced by all involved in the process. In one trial, when I asked my associate about her response to the horrifying evidence, she responded that she was having difficulty sleeping with nightmares in which she was in danger of attack like the victim.

Nevertheless, courtrooms are not always stressful places, and on many occasions, I had to control my sense of humour and not make the comment that occurred to me. The parties and witnesses involved would be concerned if the judge appeared to be amused. Sometimes, however, I would make some gentle remark, almost always directed against myself, and never carrying the suggestion that I was not taking the case or individuals seriously, to humanise the process and lighten the atmosphere in the court.

Watching the antics of fiercely competing relatives in wills cases, was often quite entertaining and informative. In one of these cases, an elderly and frail-looking female friend of the deceased was called as a witness. She was clearly appalled that the capacity of her long-time companion in an aged care home to decide who she wanted to leave her money to was being challenged by greedy relatives. When she entered the witness box and was handed the bible to be sworn, she said, 'You want me to take an oath to tell the truth', her gaze and sweeping arm encompassing everyone in room with obvious disgust as she continued with real venom, 'just like all these people here'. When counsel for the claimants asked her for her occupation, she responded that she was a pensioner, and what would he expect at her age. He then asked what that was. She said that she was obviously well above pension age and that, in any event, it was none of his business. He looked at me to intervene but I said nothing, sharing her general view of the unedifying performances of the people involved. She was a smart and dangerous witness who was quickly excused from the court. Although she gave little evidence, she was a powerful advocate for her old friend.

I had been connected for some years with a group of long-distance runners from a local athletics club, none of whom had any connection with the law. We would meet most days after work on a racecourse not far from my home for a typical training session of twelve to sixteen kilometres. This provided an important break for me, particularly at the end of a day that had been intellectually or emotionally demanding. Trials are human processes, and it is important for the judge to recognise the impact of the evidence and personal interactions viewed from different perspectives of those directly involved or affected by what has happened as well as the concerns of the wider community. Courts are foreign and inherently intimidating environments for most people and attention has to be given to conducting the proceedings as far as possible in a manner that can be seen to be fair and enable them to cope.

During my time at the bar and the years I sat as a trial judge or dealt with parole issues, I became so accustomed to dealing with the physical consequences of violence that in one trial my initial response was surprise when one of the jurors fainted during a video presentation of the deceased's injuries. However, I found myself becoming increasingly sensitive to the terrible pain and wastage of life and potential that I observed on an almost daily basis and still avoid watching films or theatrical performances that portray personal distress. The more realistic the plot of a play or film, and the better it is presented, the more uncomfortable I become as my mind fills with images of some of the people and situations I have had to deal with. Engagement for a few hours in the self-satisfying pseudo empathy on which so many dramas are based has no appeal for me.

The only person I could confide in about such matters was Dawn. I recall one trial in particular where we discussed this impact.

The accused had been found guilty by a jury of the murder of his infant child and the attempted murder of his wife who was seriously injured: one of her arms had to be amputated. He had anaesthetised her with ether to which he had access in his work before placing the baby beside her in their bed and setting a fire that would ignite after he had left the house and arrived at his workplace. She was awakened by the pain of her burning arm and, unaware of the presence of the baby, staggered confused from the room which became engulfed in flames. The motive for this crime was the wish of the accused to rid himself of obligations to them and to start a new life with a woman he had met while working for a short time in the United States.

It was a dreadful case, and I was effectively debriefing after imposing sentence while we were having dinner when Dawn pointed out we had to be careful not to become overwhelmed by the situations each of us had to deal with. They could not be allowed to compromise our relationship with each other or with our daughters.

Not only my work but also that of Dawn gave rise to this potential. As a social worker in the area of physical rehabilitation and mental health, she was dealing with some severely disabled and emotionally vulnerable people. One afternoon, when I called her at the Centre where she worked to make arrangements for something or other of little consequence, I was told by a colleague that she could not come to the phone because she was trying to talk one of the clients out of committing suicide. Altogether, it took her about eight hours to resolve the situation and arrange for continuing care. When she arrived home exhausted at about midnight, she asked me about the reason for my call. It seemed so trivial I simply said it didn't matter.

As might be expected, some of the cases attracted controversy, and my decisions were subject to public criticism. Usually, I was well aware when the outcome would not be well received or popular, and sometimes did not like the result myself. However, it would have been a betrayal of my oath of office to determine a case based on how I would have preferred to see it resolved or to tailor my findings or reasons to ensure broad approval. Although unpleasant, the legal system must be open to this kind of public scrutiny and accountability.

Judges recognise that they are not, and must not be, immune from criticism. They represent the community, but in its adherence to the fundamental values inherent in the rule of law. This does not mean that the realities of the situation are to be ignored but rather that, while cases have to be considered on their individual circumstances, this must be done in the context of the central concepts and values underpinning our system.

Justice is both a fundamental human need and an aspiration to be pursued, but it is ephemeral and only sensed in time and context. There will inevitably be situations where, viewed from the conflicting perspectives of the people involved, a reasonable outcome would require different decisions, with priority being given to different factual considerations or values. Judges can only do their best to achieve an acceptable balance as generally perceived by the community they represent, but must do so within the framework of law and principles binding them.

THE ADULT PAROLE BOARD

I was appointed as Deputy Chair of the Adult Parole Board about six months after commencing as a judge. From the time of its establishment in the 1950s, there was a widely held view in the Supreme Court that involvement in this type of activity was inappropriate because it merged the judicial and executive functions relating to sentencing. In my mind, this has always been a distinction of doubtful validity, and there was always some tension within the Court as a consequence. The situation was made more difficult by the ever-present risk of controversy associated with parole decisions that some judges saw as possibly reflecting adversely upon the Court.

In my experience, judges are generally uncomfortable about activities that may be viewed as non-judicial in character, particularly when they have the potential of attracting controversy. They dislike acknowledging that the distinction between the exercise of executive and judicial power inherent in the notion of the separation of powers is no more problematic in relation to sentencing than when applied to much of their decision-making.

There are impressionistic responses and value and priority assessments underneath almost all judgements. The law governing an area is very seldom a clear-cut set of rules that can be mechanically applied. Judges like to be seen as totally objective in the application of legal principle and their fact-finding, but they engage in a human process and with human tools. It is not always clear to the judges themselves why they have arrived at their views of the evidence or their interpretation or application of principle.

I regard my involvement in the work of the Parole Board as being at least as important, if not more so, than most of my normal trial court work. Judges regularly assert that sentencing is by far the most difficult of their tasks, but in my experience the decision to release on parole was sometimes much more worrying. Sentencing is essentially concerned with the legal system's response to past conduct, although the prospects for the future must also be considered. Parole decisions are principally directed to the future, bearing in mind what has occurred in the past. A sentencing judge fixes a period that must be served in prison but allows for the exercise of discretion to release upon its expiry. There is always a balance of risk assessment in the decision to grant or deny release on parole: setting a prisoner free at the end of their sentence without any support to facilitate reintegration into the community on the one hand, and the earlier release of a potentially dangerous individual on the other.

Our decisions to grant parole to notorious offenders were sometimes unpopular and the subject of media criticism, and I occasionally had to defend or explain them publicly. While this could be quite unpleasant, the community was entitled to know that the Board had acted responsibly. To assist in this process, both Government and Opposition parliamentarians as well as media representatives attended Board meetings.

Over the seventeen years of my involvement in this work, I interviewed several thousand prisoners and parolees. They ranged from those whose conduct could be clearly understood, when considered against their backgrounds of disadvantage, to the seriously dangerous and truly evil. It did not trouble me that prisoners tried to mislead or exaggerate in these hearings, and they were not always rejected on that basis. They were, after all, trying to persuade the Board to grant their release and wanted to present themselves as well as they could. Although many presented as manipulative and prison-wise, I have commented to others who seemed to have had no insight whatever into their behaviour or how they appeared that, 'You have not even worked out what lies to tell me, putting to one side whether you could persuade me to believe them.'

The lies or exaggerations of the different prisoners could be informative. Some were pathetic in their naivety, more reflective of their general low functioning than a sophisticated attempt to mislead, while others manifested cunning rather than any intention to integrate into normal society. I was often asked whether I was fooled by any of the prisoners that I interviewed, and would respond 'almost certainly, but only if they were skilful and then, of course, I would not find out until they were caught again'.

Many appeared to have been doomed from the outset. One prisoner, when asked whether he had family support, misunderstood the question, which was directed to his prospects on release, and happily announced he had two brothers and an uncle in gaol that he could call upon if he encountered trouble. Another, when asked the same question, responded, 'It's family support that put me here.' He said that on his previous release from prison, he was met by his mother in the parking lot with a parcel of celebratory drugs. A third said, 'Judge, you know my father.' I replied, 'I knew your grandfather.'

The process of personally interviewing all eligible prisoners and at various stages of their sentences was demanding, and many of the interviews were extremely unpleasant. I have heard remarkably imaginative and sometimes highly entertaining descriptions of my heritage, personal behaviours and physical characteristics, almost none of which were flattering. However, I was always conscious of the advice of my predecessor in the role, Sir John Starke, that I should not be bothered by the abuse of an unsuccessful applicant as

I could hardly expect them to like me.

Although there were threats made by disappointed prisoners, and it was always possible they could be carried out, usually they were seen as an outburst of frustration and not regarded as a significant problem. The closest I came to direct violence in the course of an interview occurred during one prison visit when I was in danger of being hit in the face with a large cream sponge cake. It had been placed in the room by a member of the prison staff and incautiously left on a side table. I was outlining the Board's reasons for denying a prisoner's release when he became agitated and repeatedly glanced at the cake. I was effectively trapped behind a table as he seemed to be debating whether to throw it. He regained his composure and instead slammed the door on his way out. We had the cake for morning tea.

Generally, I encountered little difficulty in these interviews as I followed a few basic rules. These included—to the consternation of the gaol authorities, who were concerned about the possibility of an attack or a hostage situation—my refusal to have prison officers within hearing range and insistence upon the removal of handcuffs and other physical restraints during the hearings. In only a handful of cases of very violent and unstable prisoners, did the Board depart from this approach. To avoid the impression of arbitrariness in our decision-making, consistency in the application of principle and the provision of adequate explanation were vital. Regardless of their own disregard of the law or how badly they had treated those around them, the prisoners generally were well informed about their eligibilities and deeply affronted by any suggestion that they may have disentitled themselves to release on the expiration of the minimum period fixed by the courts. Some became very angry when we said that, in view of their histories, we were not prepared to rely on their earnest assurances.

We preferred to have at least two interviews with the prisoners and sometimes, in the case of those serving long sentences, there would be several. The questions asked by the Board members in interviews were based on extensive knowledge and experience in the criminal justice system, a range of reports and the prisoner's criminal history file. Often, the language used was blunt and direct but usually effective in communicating our expectations and concerns.

Over the years involved in dealing with parole issues, I encountered some extraordinary individuals and life histories. One young man was only fourteen when he and his ten-year-old sister had been orphaned. They lived for a short time with relatives, who decided they would be placed in State care. Rather than be separated, the two children ran away and lived on the streets until they joined up with a group of other young people. The young man made sure his sister continued at school, and he earned money whenever and however he could. He was proud that he had always looked after her until she reached adulthood and that she was now married and had a good job. When I asked how his life had turned out so differently from hers and how he had become involved with drugs and crime, he responded simply that, while he was looking after her, there was no one to look after him.

Another, on all indications, had been making serious endeavours to remain drug and crime free until his mother's partner murdered her by dousing her in petrol and setting it alight. He wanted to stay in prison so that he could eventually be near the man and kill him.

A few, who did not want to be considered for parole, were so institutionalised after years of incarceration that release into a community in which they felt they had no place was a frightening prospect. One, who had been granted parole after serving a long sentence, had arranged to meet his daughter who he had not seen since she was a young child. He became terrified at the prospect as he thought about the lost years and what he could say to her, and so he got off the bus in which he was travelling to her home. After buying a knife from a nearby shop, he held up a chemist's shop on the other side of the road and then waited at the bus stop for the police to arrest him so he could return to prison.

Female prisoners were, with few exceptions, severely damaged. Most had backgrounds of sexual exploitation and violence, and little expectation that things would ever be better for them. Sadly, with little education and limited, if any, external supports available, that was too often the reality. While their relapse into crime could not be predicted—although it sometimes seemed to be highly likely—they were almost certainly destined for lives of hardship. There were never sufficient supports available to assist them.

A woman who came before the Board with this typical history had been born in prison and was pregnant when she became eligible for parole. She had been associated through her family with crime and criminals all her life and had served several periods of imprisonment. From the Board's perspective, her prospects of successful reintegration were almost negligible. However, our principal concern was to try to break the cycle and avoid the baby being born in a gaol. Shortly after her release, both died in a motor accident while she was affected by drugs.

There were, nevertheless, some remarkable examples of genuine rehabilitation. Three, in particular, remain imprinted on my memory. The first, a female prisoner who struggled to create a better life for herself and her young child, was released on parole against all the indications in her background and her gaol history. After interviewing her in prison, we had come to the view that a turning point had been reached and she was genuine in her intentions. The likelihood of success was small, but we judged it was almost certainly then or never. We were correct in our assessment, and she settled down with the child in a country town. Sometime later, she refused to cooperate with a former criminal associate who wanted her to support a false alibi in relation to a murder with which he was charged. She was determined to separate herself from her former life and informed the police of this approach. In retaliation, one of his associates shot her to death as she slept in her bed beside the child.

The second was a recidivist offender with a long history of imprisonment. His situation was drawn to my attention by the Governor of the country gaol, where he was serving his latest sentence, when I arrived there for a parole hearing. He told me that the man had approached him three months before in a state of extreme distress seeking compassionate leave for a day. He had been visited by his wife, who was living in poor conditions in a decrepit house not far from the prison. Their infant child had been bitten on the face by a rat as he slept in his cot. The leave was granted, and the prisoner was accompanied by a prison officer, who worked with him over a weekend, blocking rat holes and setting baits.

When he returned, he was seen to have changed. According to the Governor, he waited anxiously for the Parole Board visit, clumsily writing draft after draft of what he wanted to say to us. I had never encountered anyone who was as obviously terrified as he was when he entered the room clutching his piece of paper. We made the order for his release, and he left. A short time later, we became aware of a sound outside. He was curled up underneath the window sobbing uncontrollably into the grass. He was so ashamed of the position in which he had placed his wife and children that the pattern of his life was broken, and he was never again seen in the system.

The third involved a prisoner who, in his early twenties, had been convicted of some very serious crimes for which, in total, he had served fifteen years. He was released on parole but quickly linked up with some other released prisoners and engaged in a couple of factory break-ins. He was charged and released on bail. Due to court delays, it was another eighteen months before he was returned to prison. At first glance, his prospects for further parole were not favourable. In explanation, he said that the only people with whom he had any social contact were other former prisoners. After his release on bail, he decided his future was bleak unless he separated from them and the life that they represented. By the time he was sentenced for the break-ins, he had held a heavy labouring job handling concrete for over a year, had married and wanted to raise a family.

The stakes were high for him. If we refused or deferred parole because of his early breach, he would have to serve a substantial part, if not all, of another five years. But we were aware of the initial difficulties encountered by most prisoners on release after long periods in custody and the lack of adequate support systems for them. Also, he had shown evidence of a real endeavour to reintegrate and had done all he could. So, we decided to release him immediately. The meeting continued for several hours and it had been raining for most of that time. As we left, we were approached by the prisoner, who had been huddling soaking wet against the wall outside, waiting to thank us for giving him a chance. He also made it.

Another case involved a prisoner who had arranged for his sentence to be transferred from New South Wales so he could be closer to his family. He had been convicted in that State for a series of burglaries, and an extremely long term of imprisonment had been imposed. At that time, there was a difference between the two States in the system of remissions applicable, which meant he was entitled to consideration two years earlier in Victoria. However, the Board generally adopted the approach that the minimum period required to be served in the State where the sentence was imposed would apply.

I have never been able to identify what influenced our decision, but somehow this did not seem right in his case, and we decided to grant him parole at the earlier time. When he was informed, he broke down and sobbed, thanking God that his ordeal was over and muttering to himself that he was innocent. He kept repeating about his wife, 'And she is still waiting, and she is still waiting'. It was an emotional moment, and he sounded genuine, but as prisoners frequently acknowledged, 'If you believe what they say, there are no guilty people here.' And so, I was dubious. About three years later, it emerged in Royal Commission hearings in New South Wales that his conviction had been based on the perjured evidence of two corrupt detectives, presumably to protect the real offenders. He actually was innocent and, if we had followed our usual practice, he would have been imprisoned for, at least, two further years.

Of course, the process did not always, or indeed often, result in such dramatic changes and favourable outcomes. When dealing with offenders whose behaviour patterns were well entrenched, it was saddening to conclude that little was likely to change. On any reasonable assessment, some had to be regarded as seriously dangerous, and the community had to be protected from them. Often, it was not difficult to see the impact of their truly awful backgrounds but we had no means of recreating lost childhoods and undoing the profound damage that they had suffered. We had to deal with the consequences.

Imprisonment of young offenders for long periods is almost always problematic. Many of them come from dysfunctional families, have been subjected to physical abuse, introduced to alcohol and drugs at an early age, and are uneducated, except, of course, in the skills required to survive in a juvenile institution and criminal milieu. They have not undergone the processes of physical and social development in what we would regard as a normal healthy environment, and gain their status and identity among their peers from their criminal behaviour.

Few, to my observation, tend to see themselves as a member of the broader community that, based on their personal experiences of interactions with government authorities and betrayal by those upon whom they ought to have been able to rely, they view as hypocritical. They tend to identify with each other on the basis of common social histories and institutional experiences, viewing themselves as outside and effectively excluded from mainstream relationships and aspirations.

Little thought is needed to appreciate that adjustment to a community in which a young person had never lived for a substantial period as a child, teenager or young adult can be extremely difficult. This has been recognised for a long time now and, while there are repeated statements of concern, the easily accessible and adequate support and encouragement that are necessary if they are to make the transition is seldom available.

Most of the young men I encountered in Parole Board hearings had backgrounds of that kind and would approach us with cynical appraisal, discounting the possibility that we might have some appreciation of their situation and be genuinely trying to divert them from proceeding further down their self-destructive paths.

However humane and well managed they may be, detention for a lengthy term in a prison and juvenile institution is almost certainly damaging. A former superintendent of our main juvenile correction centre told me that the best he could hope for was that the 'kid won't go out worse than he came in'. Unfortunately, we could confidently expect to continue to see them until they developed much greater insight and maturity. The hope was that, when and if this did occur, it would not be too late. Although I hated acknowledging the likely outcome, there were many for whom I felt the die had already been cast, sometimes by them but much more frequently *for* them.

Criticism of unpopular parole decisions was not a matter of great concern—it came with the job. The central objective had to be to ensure that it was not justified and that our assessments and decisions were soundly based. Much more troublesome was the possibility that, if we were wrong in our assessment of the danger posed by an individual, innocent people might suffer.

The Parole Board was engaged in risk management with potentially catastrophic consequences, and considerable care was therefore required. Public safety was a central consideration; the Board had to consider the nature and degree of risk posed by the individual and whether it was more likely to be reduced by release under supervision or continued incarceration for the remainder of the prisoner's sentence. While they can be of assistance, sometimes with a high level of probability, no formulae or tests could accurately predict the future behaviour of any specific person. We gained considerable assistance from their personal and criminal histories, the kinds of behaviours they had engaged in, and the insights gained by psychologists and others who had encountered them. Past behaviour and demonstrated traits are still by far the most reliable predictors of the future. Personal assessment by a panel of experienced Board members also has an important part to play. Accordingly, I regarded it as essential that all eligible prisoners be interviewed before decisions were made.

Many were seen several times during their sentences. The process was both labour and resource intensive, but considered a necessary supplement to the documentary and other information available. Fortnightly meetings were held in the various prisons for this purpose. As part of the monitoring process, parolees were required to attend meetings for a warning or revocation if their compliance with conditions was unsatisfactory. Regrettably, this level of supervision by the Board controls was later regarded as excessive.

Sex offenders were the most challenging cohort to deal with as in many cases they continued to lie or attempt to justify appalling conduct. Apparently forgetting that the Board would check the records, we even had prisoners assuring us that, although innocent, they had been induced to plead guilty by their lawyers when they had been convicted by a jury after a full trial.

Most were held in two institutions that the Board would visit two or three times each year, and we would usually interview around one hundred prisoners over three days. Over the years that I was engaged in this work I conducted, at minimum, two thousand such interviews. It was always an awful experience. I have dealt with parents and grandparents—male and female—who have either abused their own children in terrible ways or made them available to sexual predators. There were individuals who, in the course of an interview, made the extraordinary claim that they had been seduced by sexually aware seven-year-old children. Throughout these meetings, it was necessary to keep reminding myself I was dealing with an aberrant element in our society and that people generally did not behave in this fashion.

Many times, it became apparent that sex offenders had been sentenced for only a tiny fraction of their crimes. Commonly, the victims had been abused so often and for so long they were unable to identify more than a few specific occasions or be prepared to disclose fully the extent of the cruelty they had suffered. Although perpetrators of sex offences sometimes claimed to be remorseful, seldom did I gain any sense of the presence of genuine empathy, and more than a few seemed to be quite comfortable with their behaviour.

Most resisted acknowledging the seriousness of what they had done and accepting personal responsibility for its consequences, and tried to avoid undertaking programs that required them to do so. Some argued that the restrictions on child sex were not necessary as it was not inherently damaging and that the harm experienced by victims was occasioned by the existence of cultural taboos that induced feelings of guilt.

Rather than participate, prisoners often preferred to lose the possibility of parole in order that they could continue to assert their innocence of wrongdoing, even in the face of overwhelming evidence. This was important to them because they could return to their families and claim to have been subjected to terrible injustice. It enabled many of the men who offended against their own daughters to continue their relationships with the rest of their families who chose, often for reasons of convenience, to treat the victims as liars.

VICTORIA UNIVERSITY

After almost forty years of trial court work as a barrister and judge and then sixteen years of involvement with the Parole Board, I was more than happy to relinquish these roles on my appointment to the Court of Appeal in 2001. This not only represented a further advancement for me, but new challenges.

That year, I also assumed the role of Chancellor of Victoria University. My interest in education, and particularly the increased opportunities that it could provide for the disadvantaged in our community, stemmed, in part, from my own background but, also importantly, from many years of exposure to the terrible wastage of potential that had resulted from their absence. I had acted for, dealt with and interviewed thousands of men and women in our criminal justice system, and often wondered what they may have made of their lives if they had seen themselves as having any realistic chance of changing their situation.

Although its history commenced in 1916, Victoria University had been established as a single entity only ten years earlier by the merger of a number of existing post-secondary training bodies in the western region of Melbourne. It is a dual sector institution, conducting courses at both the TAFE (Trade and Further Education) and higher education (university degree) levels. The new university had been given a specific mandate to contribute to educational opportunity and provide a realistic pathway for aspiration in the largely neglected western region of Melbourne. But there were many challenges: the most significant being that it was never adequately funded and always struggled to perform this role.

Just a few weeks after I commenced, the Vice-Chancellor sought my advice. He was concerned about the possibility that an extensive and ongoing fraud was being perpetrated by some senior members of staff. It was suspected that there had been long-standing corruption in the tendering processes adopted within one of the institutions that now made up the university, and that the staff members involved were still engaged in these practices. This raised management issues that would require careful handling because the allegations may have been unfounded and malicious.

As an immediate step, I directed some changes be made to the accountability processes and that an external accounting firm be engaged to conduct a more intensive audit. When it became clear that a problem did exist, the matter was referred to the police. A lengthy investigation was undertaken, and considerable time elapsed before charges were laid and several individuals were convicted.

When I started in the role, there was tension between the TAFE and higher education sectors, and also some residual dissatisfaction within the staff of the previously separate entities to the merger, each seeming to consider they were diminished in status by association with the others. These tensions remained an ongoing problem for most of the time I was involved. Eventually, there was much greater appreciation across the university of the special opportunities presented by the combination of higher and vocational education, not only for the institution generally but, more importantly, for the students. It allowed for multiple entry and exit points in the various study areas and for transition between the sectors in related fields.

In common with tertiary education institutions generally, support through public funding was effectively reduced for Victoria University which experienced an increasing need to secure additional income by commercialising its operations. A number of 'less important' courses were discarded and increased pressure placed on those that did not directly relate to the job market or had small enrolments. Although I understood the economic realities within which the university had to operate, I was always uncomfortable with this development. Universities as centres of learning and academic exploration for a society have an important but seldom fully appreciated role in encouraging a wider pursuit of knowledge than the provision of training for its workforce. Access to education at all levels is essential to the proper functioning of a modern, economically viable, democratic society and the avoidance of the development of a generational disadvantaged underclass.

The approach to funding adopted by successive governments, requiring an increased level of contribution by students who were viewed as the primary beneficiaries of higher and trade education rather than the community as a whole, created particular difficulties for Victoria University. Little allowance was ever made at a Commonwealth or State level for the necessary additional supports for our students, who were often commencing their studies at a considerable disadvantage. The university also had to compete for students and research funding with long-established institutions with far more resources. Rather than receiving additional government assistance to ensure genuine competition and reduce this disparity, the reverse happened.

Another consequence of the increasing emphasis on a more corporate administration model was pressure to convert the large university council, which had student and staff union representation, into a smaller body more akin to a company board. I had a different view of the role and responsibilities of our educational structures, and I continued to resist these changes throughout my time there. Shortly after I ceased being Chancellor, they were made.

Despite those problems, I enjoyed my involvement with Victoria

University, especially my contacts with the many dedicated and highly skilled staff members engaged in academic disciplines that I would never otherwise have encountered. Dawn and I participated in many great occasions, including the local and overseas graduations, with happy students and proud families. I particularly liked my trips to China where I went several times to meet with senior education and other officials in different parts of the country where we conducted courses and met with judges at the highest level of their rapidly evolving legal system. Law schools had been closed for a turbulent period of about ten years in the 1970s and 80s, called variously the Cultural Revolution and the Great Catastrophe, so new relationships and education programs had to be developed for the expanding private economy and international trade.

I continued as Chancellor until my retirement from the Court of Appeal in 2009.

THE COURT OF APPEAL AND BEYOND

I was appointed to the Court of Appeal a little over five years after its establishment in 1994. A number of judges and members of the legal profession expressed surprise that I would leave the position of Principal Judge in the criminal area and the drama of high-profile trials with which I had long been associated for the seemingly staid deliberations and judgement writing of the appellate jurisdiction. But after almost twenty-five years at the bar engaged in trial work and then another sixteen as a presiding judge, I was eager for change. Having reached the age of sixty and qualifying for a judicial pension, I had been vaguely contemplating retirement from the Court and, taken in conjunction with my new role at Victoria University, this appointment represented the commencement of another phase in my life.

Far from being tedious, the work was fascinating and important. As the judgements of the Court of Appeal constitute the final decisions in all except a tiny percentage of cases that proceed to the High Court, they are of immense importance to those directly involved, and to the community through the standards and principles they establish. They set precedents that bind all lower courts and tribunals in the State hierarchy, so enormous care is taken in their preparation. The judges involved meet and debate—sometimes strongly—as they interpret legislation and endeavour to apply the principles and accepted notions of justice on which our system is based, to new problems in a rapidly changing social and legal environment.

In some ways, the role was less demanding than that often performed by a judge in handling a complex or demanding civil or criminal trial, where the same issues arise, but must be dealt with in the course of an ongoing contest where there can be a wide range of practical and administrative matters that have to be handled and under much greater time constraints. By the time that a case is being heard at the appeal level, the questions to be decided are confined, usually within an accepted evidentiary and factual framework, and there is much more support and time available to the court to answer them.

From the perspective of hard-working trial judges, appeal courts have been said to operate like bandits who hide in the hills and watch battles on the plains beneath and then, when they are over, descend and massacre the wounded. As a former trial judge, I have more than a little sympathy for this view. A criminal trial develops its own atmosphere and dynamic, and the background against which evidence is given and assessed by a jury or judge at trial level is vastly different.

Some of the disadvantages under which appellate courts operate in dealing with issues of fact, and the manner in which the judge has instructed the jury or ruled on evidence, have certainly been reduced by the availability of video recordings of proceedings but they are not been completely removed.

Based on my experience of more than fifty years of work in and around courts, I do not accept that a single judge hearing a trial, or two or three appeal court judges, are more likely to be correct in their determination of questions of fact than twelve members of the community who bring a wide range of individual experiences and personalities into the jury room and independently reach a unanimous conclusion. Rather than reduce the role of citizens in our legal system, I have long been of the view that what I consider is the institutional distrust underlying many of the rules governing our trial processes needs revision.

My colleagues in the Court of Appeal were all exceptional lawyers, conscious of the nature and responsibility of their role and concerned that their decisions were based in principle as well as appropriate in the circumstances. Most of the time, there was little disagreement, and few dissenting judgements were given. Usually, one of the three judges constituting the bench dealing with an appeal would prepare a draft for consideration by the other members and a final version would be agreed upon.

I have no doubt that, in the not-too-distant future, the fact-finding processes we employ in our system of justice, the legal principles we currently accept—mostly without challenge—and our understandings of crime and personal responsibility, will be perceived as primitive. Much of what we do is already being reconsidered in view of societal changes and the insights gained through modern research techniques. I would not now accept many of the propositions or policy justifications underlying our processes with the degree of confidence that I had for almost all of my time working in the legal system. This is not a source of embarrassment, nor does it diminish my sense of the value of the work I have done in my various roles, but simply recognition of the developments that are continually occurring and the new knowledge and insights being gained.

Justice is not only an aspiration towards which human society has struggled, almost, I suspect, from its earliest days, but a necessity for its continuation. What this idea has represented over the millennia and how we have sought to achieve it have evolved according to the beliefs and circumstances of the particular communities. I have always seen my role as a judge as essentially the same as that of the many who, over that long period—whether in an elaborate courtroom or in a village hut—endeavoured to deal with issues that gave rise to potential conflict and disharmony within their communities. As ever, the obligation resting upon those entrusted with that function is to perform it with integrity and humanity, and in accordance with the law and values of the society that they represent.

While I enjoyed the demands of the role and the status I had attained, as in life generally, it was important not to take myself too seriously. Generally, my colleagues had a similar approach and directed their attention to the issues of fact and principle arising in the cases, and I liked working with them.

Judges should always bear in mind that they are highly unlikely to attain forensic immortality, and that most of what they write will be discarded or forgotten after a few years as new issues and understandings arise. Relatively few judgements receive any attention at all; it was said within the court that rarely do they have a shelf life longer than five or six years. The thousands of volumes of reported decisions in our law libraries immortalise the human capacity for error and societal change in a system that, of necessity, is always evolving. Principled adaptation and the reassessment of value priorities according to the knowledge and changing community needs are at the heart of the common law system. I was much more interested in the balance of values underpinning accepted formulations by earlier courts and their continued appropriateness than simply applying them.

Although the atmosphere in the Court of Appeal was different to the more intense experience of a criminal trial, and the debate was seemingly limited to the arcane and polite discussion of principles, it was conducted within the context of real events and consequences, not only for the particular case and people involved but for the broader community. Judgement writing occupied a great deal of my time. Because of their use as precedents, the potential for misunderstanding had to be avoided as far as possible. They were formally structured using language sanctioned by long usage and containing few variations in style.

I remained in the Court of Appeal until just before my date of compulsory retirement in October 2009. Fifty-four years had passed since I entered Melbourne University as a teenager and almost twenty-five years since I became a judge. Although I had been involved in many other activities over the years, with few exceptions they had been connected with or arisen from my work in the law.

It now seemed all behind me, and for a short time, I felt lost and depressed. This is a common experience for retirees, but I had naively believed that knowing it could happen would protect me from it. After I finished painting every room in our home, it was clear I would need to find something to do that I considered worthwhile and would allow me to contribute my experience. The answer arrived about three months later.

In extraordinary circumstances, a young man had been convicted of rape on the basis solely of the finding of his DNA on a contaminated test swab obtained in the course of the examination of a woman who it was thought may have been the subject of sexual assault. She had been found lying unconscious on the floor of the toilet in a night club catering for people of forty years and above in an outer suburb of Melbourne, having gone to the night club with some relatives. How she came to be where she was found was unknown as she had no memory of what had happened. The most likely explanation, it later emerged, was that she had passed out after ill-advisedly consuming a combination of alcohol and prescribed medication. She was taken to a hospital where tests were performed to determine the cause of her collapse and, in particular, whether she may have been the subject of a sexual assault and perhaps, given a 'date rape' drug. DNA swabs were taken in an unfortunately contaminated environment that implicated a nineteen-year-old Somali teenager living with his family many kilometres away.

There was no evidence that the young man had been present in the night club on that night or that he was even aware of it. The likelihood that he may have been there was remote for several reasons, including the improbability that a young dark-skinned teenager would have gone to a night club attended by much older people on his own, have entered and left without being observed, and while there met, drugged and raped his victim in an unknown location. He had been imprisoned for over a year when it became clear that he was undoubtedly innocent of any crime, and I was appointed by the Attorney-General to conduct an inquiry into how this miscarriage of justice had occurred.

What emerged was a disheartening picture of the unthinking processing of the case against him at every stage that resulted in serious injustice not only for the young man and his family, but also the victim, who was led to believe for over three years that she had been drugged and raped while unconscious. There was no indication in the materials I examined or the many interviews I conducted that any of those involved in the investigation or subsequent legal processing of allegation ever noticed that it was hopelessly misconceived. Total reliance was placed upon the DNA evidence which was never seriously queried and attributed magical infallibility, although it stood in stark contrast to everything else known. The inability to provide even a scenario of how, when and where the crime had been committed was treated as being of no consequence.

A remarkable but simple prosecution case was advanced. Although there was no other evidence of any kind that a sexual assault had been committed or even could have taken place, and nothing to connect the accused with either the victim or location at any time, the jury was urged to conclude that the presence of a minute quantity of his DNA on a swab taken in the course of the examination of the victim was sufficient proof that she must have been raped and that he was the perpetrator.

From my perspective, it was particularly disturbing that, for the young man to be found guilty of a crime that had never been committed and in circumstances where the existence of a possible problem with the evidence should have been apparent from the outset, the system had to fail at every stage. I made a number of recommendations that I considered would improve the system and thus avoid a similar travesty. With one exception, they were accepted by the Government and subsequently implemented.

Since then, I have undertaken several inquiries or reviews. My longest such engagement was as senior advisor to the Victorian Parliament's Community and Social Development Committee's investigation into the sexual and physical abuse of children in non-government institutions.

This was the first major investigation undertaken into this problem in Australia, although more limited inquiries had been pursued in other States, and contributed to the establishment of a wide-ranging Commonwealth Royal Commission. Although the Committee was constituted by representatives of the Government and Opposition political parties, and tensions could have been anticipated, it could not have functioned more successfully or harmoniously. All members and the staff involved were dedicated to discovering and exposing the extent of the problem, and developing recommendations to address the issues that emerged. This was reflected at all stages of the process and particularly in the confidential sessions, where the members provided sensitive support to the nervous victims as they described what had happened to them and its consequences.

The institutional hypocrisy evident within the leadership of major religious organisations, and their determination to protect the status and reputations in total disregard of the terrible damage to the many victims over decades, was sickening. The Catholic church hierarchy, in particular, expressed feigned surprise at the disclosure of the endemic nature of a problem which they had been well aware of for decades, and, once confronted with it, their primary objective was to limit the consequent damage to their reputation and finances. Almost all of the Committee's recommendations were adopted by Parliament on a bipartisan basis. We were all proud of what we were able to achieve.

The other investigations in which I have been engaged were varied, and include three that, for various reasons were sensitive—the first of them arose from allegations of a conflict of interest in a possible inappropriate relationship between the Director of Public Prosecutions and a young staff member. Considerable ill-feeling had developed within the organisation when the staff member had been quickly advanced and promoted in preference to a number of others who were seen as at least equally if not more experienced and qualified.

The second related to problems that had emerged in the witness protection system operated by Victoria Police and followed the murder in their home of a potential witness and his wife and that of a notorious criminal in prison. On this occasion, a redacted version of my report was released publicly and some changes made to the legislation and processes.

The third was directed to the making of orders (called suppression orders) by judges preventing the public dissemination of information given in court proceedings. The frequency and terms of these orders had been the subject of media complaints for a long time with an earlier attempt to deal with the issue by legislation being largely unsuccessful. There has been increased attention to this matter following numerous breaches of orders relating to proceedings against the Catholic Cardinal, George Pell, for sexual offences committed on two altar boys. The difficulties presented by orders of this kind have, to some extent, now been addressed in new statutory provisions based on the adoption of some of my recommendations.

I have enjoyed the semi-investigative dimension of this kind of work and the practical problem-solving involved. It is a little disappointing, but unavoidable, that some of my reports on these matters either remain confidential or have been released to the public in a redacted form.

Dawn and I are happy. She has been actively engaged in the practice and academic learnings of her profession, and keeps up to date with developments, both local and international, in a range of related disciplines. I have encountered many in my own work who presented themselves as having years of experience when it seemed to me that they had one year which had been continually repeated without acquiring any greater depth in their understanding. That definitely could not be said of Dawn. We are still able to travel and have some wonderful trips together. I have continued my interest in long-distance running and completed a marathon just before my eightieth birthday.

Our daughters have grown into strong and principled professional women with their own children. Watching them all grow and 'closing their own doors' has been our greatest reward.

Where to now?

We still have work to do, places to visit and challenges to meet.

The tapestry of our lives is not yet complete, and I hope that quite a few more threads will be woven into it. If not, I can hardly complain.

www.ingramcontent.com/pod-product-compliance
Ingram Content Group UK Ltd.
Pitfield, Milton Keynes, MK11 3LW, UK
UKHW041950190726
13854UKWH00004B/1880

9 781925 736434